STRESS FREE

Manoj Krishna used to be a spine surgeon and left that career to start the Human Wisdom Project (humanwisdom.me). His first book, *Understanding Me, Understanding You*, was translated into four languages. He has a long-standing interest in how our minds work. He feels passionately about the need for all of us to explore and understand our inner spaces, because this awakens life-changing wisdom, which can help us understand and overcome stress. He lives in Yorkshire.

STRESS FREE

UNDERSTAND YOURSELF.
DISCOVER WISDOM.
BE FREE.

by

Manoj Krishna

ClearTree Press

Published by ClearTree Press, Yarm, England.
Cleartreepress.com

Printed and bound in Great Britain by Clays Ltd, St Ives plc

The author's website is humanwisdom.me

ISBN-13 978-0-9956833-9-6

ACKNOWLEDGEMENTS

I am grateful to the many teachers whose writings have inspired me. In particular, the writings of J. Krishnamurti (1895–1986) have been very insightful and can be found at jkrishnamurti.org.
I have mentioned several facts in the book and I am grateful to those who have collated them. I have not referenced them, but they can be easily validated through a search engine.
I am also grateful to the many friends and family members who have provided feedback and with whom I have held long discussions.

For Sanjay and Shubhada

CONTENTS

FOREWORD

I HAD BEEN A SPINE surgeon for many years. One day I was driving back from a long day of surgery and heard the sound of children screaming on the radio. A hospital they had been in had been bombed, somewhere in the Middle East. In that moment, I had an insight that I felt could make a difference and that is when I made the decision to leave medicine, write my first book, *Understanding Me, Understanding You*, and start the Human Wisdom Project – to share this understanding with others. The idea was simple. Since many of our problems including stress and conflict between different groups of people, first begin with our thinking, the solution lies in understanding ourselves and how our minds work.

With this new direction in life, I began in education, thinking that if we could educate a new generation of children with this understanding, which leads to wisdom, we could transform their lives and change the world. I made an amazing discovery. They already had this wisdom, and it was just waiting to be awakened in them. Wherever I went, the topic people always wanted me to speak about – was stress. I did some polling during these talks (using software that allows people to answer questions anonymously), and between 70–80% of people I met said that they were moderately or severely stressed, and one in three said that they had suffered a mental health problem in the previous year. I believe much of this emotional distress is avoidable if we can meet life with this wisdom.

I have shared this understanding with the people I have met over the last few years and their feedback has encouraged me to write this book, and share this with you.

It encapsulates everything I have learnt on a journey of questioning life and learning about myself, which began when I first joined medical school, 40 years ago. I read widely, and am grateful to all those human beings who have gone before, over thousands of years, who have explored the human mind and shared what they learnt. I realised on the way that real transformation comes not from following others, but from undertaking the journey of enquiry for oneself. I think it is possible for everyone to do this.

I write this book not as a specialist, but as an ordinary human being, like you, who is just asking questions of the life we live. In many ways, this was an advantage because it left me free to explore widely and not be anchored in one particular philosophy or ideology. I have applied this enquiry-based approach to the many stressful situations I have encountered over the years, both professionally and personally, and have found it transformative. It has helped me deal with people and life's challenges in a completely fresh way and avoid so much suffering as a result. You do not need a degree in psychology or philosophy to question the life you live or to benefit from the wisdom that you can discover by doing so. People who have shared the most profound insights have sometimes never been to college or university.

People ask me if I miss my surgical career, and they are surprised when I say that I do not. When you live with a passion for something, your heart is always full, wherever you are.

INTRODUCTION

Dear Reader,

Stress gets in the way of our happiness. I have spoken in over 50 institutions over the last two years, and of the many things I have learnt, one stands out to me. There is one thing that everyone wants – to be happy. Despite this, a massive 80% of us report being moderately or severely stressed. Why have we not been able to use our fantastic intellect to resolve this problem?

Some months ago, I attended an educational conference. A father stood up and spoke about his son, who had gone to university a few months before, and had never come back. He had struggled with his courses, had mental health issues, and had taken his own life. I wish I could say that this story is unique, but unfortunately, it is all too common. This and other similar stories moved me deeply. I believe that with a deeper understanding of the nature of stress, tragedies like this are avoidable.

Our suffering is very real, and so much of it is avoidable, if only we had a deeper understanding of the nature of stress, its origins in our thinking, and had strategies to manage ours intelligently. This book aims to explore and understand the origins of stress in our thinking and suggest that this understanding can help us meet life with serenity, prevent us from getting stressed in the first place, and deal with it more effectively if we do. We are also going to explore how we can respond to the stressors of life with intelligence and in such a way that we do not try and distract ourselves from our feelings using food, alcohol, or drugs, which can cause problems of their own.

This understanding of ourselves and how our minds work awakens our own intelligence and leads to wisdom. By intelligence I do not just mean being smart or being able to memorise information, but rather an intelligence that emerges from a deeper understanding of our inner spaces, from an insight into how our minds work. This intelligence is a combination of self-awareness and self-knowledge, an ability to notice our thoughts and feelings clearly, and understand the many patterns of thinking behind them. This ability to see clearly, without judgement, leads to wisdom, which can change our lives.

For myself, this wisdom is alive when I notice that I am not listening to someone because I am, instead, thinking of something I want to say. Or when, in an argument, I notice that both of us are attached to our points of view, and we are just generating more heat than light, or, finally, when I come to an understanding that though you and I may have different religious beliefs, the nature of belief is the same in both of us. It is also alive when I get hurt by something you have done, and can see that it is my own unmet expectation that is causing my pain, so the actual cause of my pain lies within myself.

All human beings share the same underlying processes or patterns of thinking. Deep down, our minds function in similar ways. For example, all of us have many emotional needs that we are not aware of, but which operate behind the scenes, shaping our thinking and our behaviour. One of them is the need to feel important, for example. If we are not made to feel important when we expect to be, we can get stressed and blame the other person for hurting us. Being aware of our sense of hurt and pausing to explore what caused it, will reveal our need to feel important operating in the background. We accept this without judgement. This awareness allows us to respond to our hurt in an intelligent way, not by blaming the other person but by asking why we want to feel important in the first place, and exploring that further. There are many similar processes of thinking that operate in the background. Understanding them and seeing how they impact our life allows us to respond to life with intelligence.

We learn to swim, so when challenges come, we do not drown. Much as we try to exert control over our lives, life is inherently unpredictable, so we have to be prepared. Monumental challenges can come at any time, take any form, and will, of course, keep coming. And with challenge comes pressure, and yes, stress – possibly more than we may feel we are capable of handling. Understanding the nature of stress is the first step in allowing us to meet the challenges of life with calm. It is like learning how to swim, so that when the challenge comes, we have the ability to swim right through it to the other side. I believe everyone is capable of observing the many hidden patterns of thinking that are behind the stress we feel. Everyone in a group who starts swimming lessons will have different levels of natural ability and will learn to swim at a different rate, but everyone eventually learns to swim.

Our current model in society for dealing with mental health problems is to say, "Shout for help if you are drowning and we will throw you a life jacket". You only get the life jacket if you are seriously in danger. Resources are limited, and sometimes there are not enough life jackets for everyone who needs them. In some situations, a drowning person is so distressed that they have no energy to shout for help.

Most people look for solutions to stress *after* it has occurred. That is natural. Sometimes the challenges of life can catch us unawares and severely limit our ability to respond in any meaningful way – or we may respond in ways that are harmful to our long-term health, by taking drugs, for example. Long-term stress can also reduce our ability to cope. When we do seek assistance, the help that is offered is usually designed to deal with the symptoms of stress rather than the root cause. Prevention is so much easier and so much more effective. Acquiring a deeper understanding of the root causes of stress in our thinking (which can help us avoid them in many cases, and respond more appropriately in others), is the focus of this book.

However, exploring the underlying causes of stress in our thinking is challenging because it means that we have to take responsibility for the stress we feel – and not blame others for it. Every instinct we have says that what we feel is someone else's fault. It is much easier for us to blame others for our stress, and if we are watchful, we will notice that this also brings a subtle form of pleasure. This book is based on the premise that though the external triggers of stress may vary, the beginnings of stress lie within ourselves, in our thinking. Stress lies in our reaction to an event and not in the event itself, though the two may appear to be linked. The benefit of taking responsibility for our feelings is that this can empower us to do something about our stress, without waiting for the situation to change.

Let me illustrate some key ideas with some analogies.

Consider the example of a traffic jam. Is it the traffic that is causing our stress, or our reaction to it? If the traffic jam was causing stress, then it would affect everyone equally. However, not everyone in a traffic jam is stressed, and those that are, experience it to different degrees. It follows that it must be our *reaction* to being stuck in traffic that is the cause. Of course, quite often our mind does not observe this distinction, and so, we instead think that it is the external situation that is the true catalyst for our feelings of distress.

Once we have established that our stress is mostly caused by our reaction to an event, the next question is – *how do we find out where that reaction comes from?*

When a car breaks down, we look under the bonnet to see what the problem with the engine is. Once we identify the cause, the solution is self-evident; the oil may need to be topped up, for example. Most car engines follow similar principles, so if I can understand how one works, I can understand them all. Similarly, when we are stressed, it is worth looking within to find out what is behind it, and once we find the root cause, the solution is clear. To look within, all we have is our intelligence. How we explore our inner spaces is key to the discoveries we will make, and that is explored in some depth in the book.

Rather than just treating the symptoms of stress, if we can find the root cause, we can end it at its root, as the following analogy makes clear.

A child has a fever and you go to see the doctor. A good doctor will understand that the fever is a symptom of an underlying disease, and by finding out what that disease is, the treatment can be targeted and effective. If a child has meningitis and you do not diagnose that accurately, it can be fatal in a few hours. Similarly, you could say stress is a symptom of a dysfunction in our thinking, and we can deal with it most effectively by understanding the actual cause. If we just treat the symptoms, the patterns of stress will keep repeating themselves in our lives.

Understanding the origins of a problem points us to the solution. Sometimes little effort is required and if a problem is seen clearly then action follows quickly. For example, we know that sunshine is essential for life, but the day we discovered that too much exposure could cause skin cancer, we automatically started applying suncream when we went to a beach. At other times, even if we see a problem clearly, more patience, perseverance, and commitment may be required to bring about sustained change. For example, if you have a well-established habit of drinking too much alcohol, then changing that needs more perseverance, but the core approach is the same. It needs us to explore the nature of our habits, how they come about and get established, and also explore the emotional needs that drinking fulfils and ask if those needs can be met in a different way. We may need to face up to an emotional pain we feel, or accept a situation as it is, or come to terms with our own emptiness, or rebuild our relationships. This may not apply in all cases, though. For example, if you are, say, being physically abused by someone else. In that case the appropriate response is to remove yourself from that situation and get help. These approaches are not prescriptive, per se; understanding the origins of a problem in our thinking presents us with options we can explore to determine the best course of action for ourselves.

One other advantage of understanding ourselves is that it becomes much easier for us to understand others, and that can improve the quality of all our relationships.

We think our stress is unique to us, but these feelings, like anger, envy, sadness, anxiety, and emotional pain, are the same in all human beings, as are the internal patterns of thinking – usually hidden from our awareness – that give rise to them. Aside from our physical appearance, the main difference between us is the content of our memory. Just as our hearts function in similar ways, the human mind also functions in the same way in all of us, but that fact is hidden from our view. You may have lost a pet, and I may have lost my job, but the feeling of sadness we feel is the same. You may be stressed because you are waiting for an exam result, and I am stressed because I am waiting for the results of a job interview, but the feeling of anxiety is the same. You may be looking forward to your next holiday, and I am looking forward to buying a new camera, but the nature of pleasure in us is the same. The internal mechanisms in our thinking that are behind our stress and sorrow are also the same. Exploring this process brings illumination, insight, and can result in a profound transformation. For example, the human mind is conditioned by all its past influences in such a way that we are usually not aware of it, and this determines our opinions and actions. Having an insight into this process can bring transformation.

In this book, I have used the widest possible meaning of the word stress, to describe the distress and pain we feel in our inner spaces. We call this by different names depending on the context, including unhappiness, stress, anxiety, sadness, or worry. Though each of us associates these words with different meanings, they are worth exploring together because they have similar roots in our thinking and they all cause emotional distress.

We are going to explore the nature of stress together. We know water has certain properties: it is transparent; it is a liquid that turns into vapour at 100 degrees Celsius at sea level, and it freezes at zero degrees. These are universal facts about water. Similarly, we can explore the universal facts about stress regardless of who suffers from it and whatever may be its cause. Our response to stress is often unconscious and follows specific established patterns that we can explore together. For example, when we are stressed, we want to escape from it because it is like a fire in our mind. We can do this in a variety of ways, some of which, like alcohol and drugs, actually make things worse in the long-term.

The internal patterns of thinking that can give rise to stress are usually hidden from our awareness. By exploring them, we can learn how to respond with intelligence. There is a crucial difference between reacting and responding to a situation. A reactive response is not thought through and may even involve violence. What does *responding with intelligence* mean? It means that we do not *react* automatically to situations. We see what is happening both inside and outside of us clearly and can *respond* in the most appropriate way to that situation. In that response, there is clarity, compassion, and often, no emotional distress. It does not mean that we are passive and do nothing in life, or do not respond to injustice or abuse when we see it, for example. Instead, we respond with vibrant intelligence and an absence of emotional distress. When we are stressed, we cannot think clearly, and our mind's capacity is limited. Responding with intelligence means that we have the energy to do the most appropriate next thing in that situation. This may mean doing nothing or taking action, but the action is not associated with fear or emotional pain.

The beauty of this approach is that no effort to change is required, the understanding itself is the driver of change. By *effort* I mean the energy you may spend 'trying not to be stressed'. All we have to do is explore and understand what is going on in our inner spaces when we get stressed. This understanding gives rise to a different type of intelligence in us, and it is this intelligence that results in change without effort. Another way to consider this is that change comes from exploring a fact, in this case, the stress itself, and not from pursuing an ideal, which is the thought that says, "I should not be stressed". I use the word intelligence in this book to mean a mind that has the ability to see itself clearly. Such clarity gives rise to wisdom. This is different from being clever, or being able to memorise and repeat knowledge, or have a number of degrees after our name, though all of these also have their place.

We know we need to eat well and exercise to look after our physical health, but how can we look after our mental health? When asked this question, we often do not know how to respond. It has rarely been explored as part of our formal education, which focused on helping us to get a job and be successful, but did little to prepare us for the emotional challenges of life. We were only taught about the world around us, but not about ourselves or how our minds work.

Beyond the emotional distress that stress causes, researchers are discovering new ways in which chronic or long-term stress can damage our physical health. It is estimated that more than half of the General Practitioner appointments in the UK are linked to emotional distress in some way. Chronic stress is associated with a shorter lifespan and is implicated in many health problems including heart disease, high blood pressure, and even cancer. If we want to protect our long-term health, it is important that we give our energy to exploring the fundamental cause of stress and to find out if we can live with a sense of peace.

NASA spends twenty billion dollars a year exploring outer space, and as a result, we have made extraordinary discoveries about our place in the universe. To begin this journey of understanding ourselves, we need to harness that sense of curiosity we have about the world around us and use it to explore our *inner* spaces. There are so many amazing discoveries to be made by exploring our inner spaces, which can transform our lives and make the world a better place. It leads to wisdom, which is essential for our happiness. This wisdom is only discovered by undertaking the journey of exploration ourselves. While there is much to be learnt from others and what can be formally taught, in the ultimate sense, there is no substitute for a direct, personal experience.

We are amazing at solving problems that we encounter in the world around us and have found cures for so many diseases. Why do we just accept the problems that emerge from our inner spaces, like stress, and assume that they have no solution? Perhaps it is because we have never even considered the possibility that a solution is possible or that there is an entire world inside us waiting to be explored, the understanding of which could transform the way we live.

We human beings are capable and ambitious when we set our minds on a particular goal. Most of these goals are in the world outside of us – to be famous, wealthy, to do something worthwhile, have great experiences, and so on. Perhaps we could bring the same energy and enthusiasm to exploring our inner spaces, and be excellent human beings who live with compassion and a sense of peace, who can meet the challenges of life without too much stress and have happy relationships.

I invite you to read this book with a spirit of learning and an open mind. This spirit of learning means being open to new ideas and willing to examine them freshly. The usual way in which our unconscious mind works is that we accept things that we already know and reject things that are different. We translate whatever we hear and try and interpret it in light of our pre-existing knowledge. Could you wake up to this process going on in the background and neither accept nor reject what is being said but examine it freshly for yourself with an open mind? This is essential if you want to get the most from this approach to understanding and dealing with stress in a new way.

You may benefit from keeping a journal as you go through the book and write your own thoughts in response to questions being explored. Writing taps into a different, more reflective part of our thinking.

Please do not accept anything you read in this book without examining it for yourself. It is only true if you see it clearly, in operation in your own life. Equally, please do not reject something because it feels different or 'impractical'. All we are doing together is exploring and understanding the origins of stress in our thinking. This clarity brings change, and that happens mysteriously, without effort. It can also help us avoid most of the common stresses in our lives and give us the tools to calmly deal with the challenges we face.

With this approach, stress becomes an opportunity to learn about the hidden machinery of thinking that causes it rather than just a problem to be endured or solved. This understanding has the potential to bring freedom.

Welcome.

YOU ARE NOT ALONE

WHEN WE ARE STRESSED, WE often feel that our feelings are unique to us, and we can feel alone in our suffering. It may be beneficial to realise that stress is extremely common and that this feeling is the same in all human beings, so that we can explore it together. It impacts our emotional, physical, and financial well-being.

In 2014, the American Psychological Association published its results on stress in the country and found that 77% of the people regularly experienced physical symptoms caused by stress, while 73% experienced *psychological* symptoms caused by stress. Also, 33% felt they had extreme stress, and 48% said that their stress had increased in the last year.

The Mental Health Foundation in the UK did an online poll of 4,619 people in 2018 and found that 74% of the people had felt so stressed that they had been unable to cope. Besides, 46% reported that they ate unhealthily or too much due to stress and 29% said that they started or increased their drinking due to stress. Further, 51% of the adults who were stressed reported feeling depressed and 61% reported feeling anxious. Of those who had felt stress at some point in their lives, 16% had self-harmed and 32% had suicidal thoughts or feelings.

The National Union of Students in the UK surveyed students and found that 78% of them reported mental health problems in the previous year, with 46% saying that their stress had impacted their quality of life.

The social network, After School, conducted an online poll on stress in the US, asking 35,878 teenagers questions about their experience of stress. They found that 45% of the teens felt stressed 'all the time'. Their leading causes of stress were relationships, teachers, parents, college, and friends. To cope with their stress, 19.65% turned to eating while 10.79% took drugs or alcohol.

The charity, Young Minds, estimates that one in ten children in the UK has a diagnosable mental health disorder, rising to one in five of young adults. In 2015, suicide was the most frequent cause of death in boys and girls between five and 19.

The polling I have conducted as part of my talks in colleges in the UK suggests that between 70–80% of the students and staff suffer from severe or moderate stress. When I ask students and teachers what they want from their life, happiness is their number one aspiration. How can people be happy with these levels of stress? Where both the teacher and student are stressed, what is the quality of the learning that is taking place?

The numbers will of course vary depending on age, type of work, economic status, and other factors, but are alarmingly high, nevertheless. Why are stress levels so high in some of the wealthiest countries in the world? Why have we just accepted stress as a normal part of life and not challenged ourselves individually and as a society to do something about it?

Stress can also have a significant economic impact on our lives because of time lost from work, and this can add to the stress we feel. Stress at work is caused by excessive workload, job uncertainty, unsocial hours, relationship issues, lack of recognition, communication problems, limited career development, and conflicting demands of work and home. It can result in loss of productivity, high levels of sick leave, employee turnover, and litigation.

In a recent EU-funded project carried out by Matrix (2013), the cost in Europe of work-related depression was estimated at €617 billion per year.

Furthermore, the Health and Safety Executive in the UK estimates that in 2017-18, 15.4 million working days were lost due to work-related stress, depression, or anxiety and this affected 595,000 workers. This equates to 57% of the working days lost to ill-health.

The economic impact of stress is not limited to the United Kingdom and Europe. The American Institute of Stress (2013) estimates that the cost of stress to US employers is more than $300 billion per year. Safe Work Australia (2012) estimated that work-related mental stress costs Australian society AU$5.3 billion annually.

Stress does not just have a financial cost. In 2015, Joel Goh and colleagues estimated that in the US, it resulted in 120,000 deaths per year.

These numbers paint a picture of the social, personal, and economic impact of stress. The aim is not to make you despondent, but to show you that you are not alone in feeling stressed and to suggest that if you commit to this journey of self-understanding and the exploration of your inner spaces, there is the possibility of avoiding many of the daily stresses of life and being able to deal with those stresses more easily when they arise.

WHY BOTHER?
STRESS DAMAGES OUR HEALTH

WHY BOTHER MAKING AN EFFORT to study the causes of stress, and finding a long-term solution to it? After all, is it not just a normal part of life which we all have to accept? Some argue that it is even good for us because it builds resilience and character. Besides the emotional pain it causes, stress can also damage our long-term health. This is sometimes overlooked because the mental anguish it can create is so distressing, and for some people, a fog they can feel lost in. I am not referring to acute stress that is short-lived, but chronic, long-term stress. Acute stress may be good for us because it prepares us to meet the challenges we face, if we are attacked, for example. There is a lot of research to suggest that long-term stress can reduce the effectiveness of our immune system, which can make us more prone to many illnesses. In this chapter, we will explore the different ways in which stress impacts our health. The good news is that despite this long list of problems that stress can cause, it is preventable, and that is the focus of this book.

SYMPTOMS OF STRESS

We are usually not aware that we are stressed because the symptoms are varied and affect us in different ways. Being aware of them is crucial so that we can then do something about it.

Of the 330 million General Practitioner medical appointments in the UK, approximately 40% are linked to a mental health issue, and this number is rising. This will be similar in other countries. Imagine the money all health systems could save if everyone was educated to respond to life's challenges in a fresh way, with serenity?

Stress affects our mind, body, behaviour, and emotions in subtle ways that are not immediately apparent. Not each symptom on its own is due to stress and may have other causes, but collectively they point to a diagnosis of chronic stress.

Linked to the body:

- Frequent colds and infections
- Low energy
- Increased heart rate
- Diarrhoea, constipation, nausea
- Headaches
- Aches and pains in muscles
- Loss of sexual desire/ability
- Clenched jaw and grinding teeth
- Skin irritations

Linked to our mind (cognitive):

- Constant worrying
- Forgetfulness
- Inability to concentrate
- Feeling pessimistic
- Poor judgement
- Nightmares

Linked to our emotions:

- Moodiness
- Being agitated
- Getting angry more easily
- Having difficulty relaxing
- Feeling lonely or isolated
- Feeling depressed or low
- Feeling overwhelmed or a feeling of losing control

Linked to our behaviour:

- Eating more, or less
- Sleeping too much or too little

- Isolating yourself from others
- Procrastinating and avoiding responsibilities
- Increased use of alcohol, cigarettes, or drugs
- Nervous habits (nail biting, fidgeting, pacing, etc.)

Do you think you may be stressed? Please do not worry because as we have seen from the statistics cited above, the majority of people around you feel the same. Acknowledging this fact is the first step in doing something about it.

PHYSICAL EFFECTS OF STRESS

Scientists have shown that chronic stress can shorten the protective caps called telomeres on the ends of our DNA. An enzyme called telomerase, which is responsible for telomere length, is reduced in people with chronic stress and cortisol exposure. Shorter telomere length is associated with faster aging of the cell. Other studies have shown that people with shorter telomeres have an earlier onset of age-related diseases, a shorter lifespan, and have a higher risk of diabetes, cancer, and heart disease.

The new science of psychoneuroimmunology is exploring how the mind and body are intimately connected and how chronic stress can reduce the effectiveness of the immune system, which in turn can make us more prone to disease – from the common cold to heart disease.

Chronic stress, which can lead to depression, results in behaviours which can damage our immune system further: like poor sleep, overeating, not enough exercise, and too much alcohol consumption. People start taking drugs as a means of dealing with the emotional pain caused by their stress, and this may also explain why drug addiction is so prevalent the world over.

Long-term stress is recognised as a risk factor in the development or exacerbation of many diseases:

- Mental illness including depression, anxiety, and personality disorders
- Cardiovascular disease including high blood pressure, abnormal heart rhythms, heart attacks, and stroke

- Obesity and other eating disorders
- Sexual dysfunction including impotence and loss of sexual desire
- Skin problems like acne, psoriasis, and eczema
- Abdominal problems including reduced appetite, gastritis, irritable bowel syndrome, and ulcerative colitis
- Structural changes in the brain including shrinkage and memory problems
- Breast cancer

The medical research available in each of these areas is vast. But in the end, presuming we all want to live long and healthy lives, these facts will likely provide ample motivation for exploring the subject of stress and finding ways of minimising it in our lives.

We eat well and exercise to look after our physical health, but what do we do to look after our mental health? We brush our teeth every day so that they remain healthy, but what do we do to stay mentally healthy?

We all have some level of stress. It is a given and a part of the human condition. Most of the long-term stress we accumulate originates in how we react to the challenges we face, and the forms that our reactions take emerge from our thinking. The key, therefore, also lies in understanding how our mind functions. We cannot always control the challenges that we will face in life, but we can do something about how we *respond* to them. We are looking to explore the hidden, automatic patterns of thinking that contribute to the undue quantity of stress that so many of us feel. Such clarity has the potential to help us avoid stress in most cases, and to respond with intelligence when faced with the challenges that life presents us every day.

TYPES OF STRESS DISORDER

Medical professionals use the word 'stress disorder' in a precise way. Four common patterns of stress disorder can occur after a traumatic event (I include these terms here so that you know what doctors are thinking, should you ever need to see one. These definitions help us to categorise our own feelings of stress should we be faced with a traumatic event in our lives):

Acute stress reaction: symptoms occur within an hour of the episode (natural disaster, severe accident, sexual assault, witnessing a violent death) and start to settle down within 48 hours. Patients also experience feelings of anger, despair, social withdrawal, and transient depression.

Post-traumatic stress disorder (PTSD): symptoms occur within six months of the traumatic experience (natural disaster, war, severe accident, witnessing a violent death, sexual assault) and can become chronic. Patients relive the experience through nightmares, avoid reminders of the event, have difficulty sleeping, and get easily startled.

Adjustment disorder: symptoms occur within a month of a major life event (divorce, job loss, physical illness) and start settling in at about six months. Symptoms may include depression, anxiety, and change in behaviour.

Furthermore, depending on how long the symptoms last, the American Psychological Association divides stress into acute, episodic acute, and chronic stress.

Acute stress: is a reaction to a short-term external event, like a car accident, or a failed driving test, or a child being upset. It is short-lived and does no permanent damage.

Episodic acute stress: is where the same event repeats itself. As in, for example, a particularly challenging relationship.

Chronic stress: is where the stress does not fade with time and can damage our health. Examples of this are people who have to deal with the challenges of poverty, unhappy relationships, challenging jobs, or long-term health problems. It is chronic stress that has the most impact on our long-term health.

MENTAL HEALTH PROBLEMS CAUSED BY STRESS

Depression, anxiety, and alcohol and drug abuse are common in patients who are stressed. Chronic stress increases the levels of the hormone *cortisol*, which has been linked to depression.

Each of these terms has precise medical meanings.

Depression: doctors diagnose depression when a patient has symptoms every day for a minimum of two weeks. These symptoms can include low mood or sadness, loss of interest or pleasure, feelings of guilt or low self-esteem, disturbed sleep or appetite, low energy, loss of sex drive, thoughts of suicide, and poor concentration. Depression is classified as mild, moderate, or severe and can occur as a reaction to life events such as unemployment, pregnancy, conflict in relationships, loss of a loved one, or physical illness. These are treated with a combination of talking therapy and medication.

Anxiety disorder: this is diagnosed when a feeling of unease, worry, or fear impacts a person's daily life. Symptoms include a sense of dread, restlessness, difficulty concentrating, disturbed sleep, irritability, and a feeling of being 'on edge'. Anxiety can result in a dry mouth, palpitations, sweating, headaches, dizziness, and nausea. Treatments include talking therapies, Cognitive Behavioural Therapy (CBT), or medication.

Substance abuse: alcohol and drug abuse, and addiction are more common among people who have a stress disorder, compared to the general population. It is a reaction to emotional pain and an attempt to dull the sensation we feel. These addictions further damage our mental and physical health.

It is helpful to know the sort of problems stress can cause so that we can avoid them if possible, and if we cannot, then know that we need to seek medical advice. The earlier we seek help, the better.

STRESS INCREASES THE RISK OF DYING

Several research studies have shown that people who are stressed have an increased risk of early death. This may be surprising to many because we often think of stress as short-term and something we cannot avoid. The research studies I have quoted below suggest that long-term stress can increase the risk of an early death by 21%, as well as increase the risk of heart disease and stroke.

Specifically, in 2012, Tom Russ and colleagues published a paper in the *British Medical Journal* outlining the results of their long-term study of 68,222 individuals, which examined the relationship between psychological distress and mortality over several years. Individuals who were considered to be psychologically distressed had a 21% increased risk of death from all causes. They also had a 22% increased risk of cardiovascular disease death, a 9% increased risk of cancer death, and a 26% increased risk of death from external causes. What fascinates me about this data is that they found that the higher the distress, the greater the mortality risk.

In 2008, Hamer and colleagues published the results of a research study in which they found an increased risk of mortality, mainly from cardiovascular disease, in 4,501 mentally distressed patients. They also used the GHQ-12 questionnaire and found that the more the distress, the higher the mortality risk.

In 2006, Nicholson and colleagues published a paper in the *European Heart Journal*, which studied the role of depression in heart disease. They analysed 21 studies and found that if people were clinically depressed, they had an increased risk of getting heart disease.

In 2011, Pan and colleagues published a paper in the *Journal of the American Medical Association*, which suggested an increased risk of stroke in patients with depression.

The mind and body are one, and disease in one affects the other. We focus on diet and exercise as a way of keeping fit and healthy, but perhaps need to give the same energy to understanding and minimising the chronic stress in our lives.

STRESS INCREASES SUICIDE RISK

The UK-based charity MIND estimates that one in five adults will consider suicide at some point in their lives. Sometimes stress causes such severe emotional distress that people feel caught in a fog of pain from which, it appears to them that there is no escape. All the normal coping mechanisms we have are eroded by the stress. The best way to address this issue is through prevention, and we can do that by living with wisdom and a vibrant intelligence which meets life's challenges in a fresh way. I have come across several instances where people reacted to an acute stressful event by taking their own lives. I knew some of them personally. None of them ever thought it could happen to them. We cannot know when life is going to present us with challenges that demand our best in dealing with them. Having this wisdom, which comes from studying ourselves and how our minds work, allows us to be prepared for these challenges and meet them in a fresh way. The studies I quote below suggest that the risk of suicide increases if we are responding to an acute trauma in our lives, and that many people who take their own lives do have a history of mental health problems. Young people are particularly vulnerable as they have not developed the skills to cope with the challenges they face, and self-harm is one way of expressing their distress.

In 2015, Gradus and colleagues published a paper in the *American Journal of Epidemiology*, analysing data from the Danish national health-care and social registers. They found that patients diagnosed with an acute stress reaction had a 24 times higher risk of death by suicide. Patients with PTSD had a 13 times greater risk of suicide.

In their 2018 report, the Centers for Disease Control and Prevention in the US noted that in 2016, there had been nearly 45,000 deaths from suicide, and this was 30% more than in 1999. It is worth noting that 54% of the people attempting suicide did not have a known mental health condition. Relationships, substance abuse, health and financial problems were reported to be the leading causes.

Self-harm is another expression of stress, especially in young people. In 2018, the Children's Society, a UK-based charity, published its seventh Good Childhood report. They found that 22% of the girls and 9% of the boys were self-harming, which included drug and alcohol abuse and physical self-harming. Children who self-harm are at an increased risk of suicide later on in life.

I believe every suicide is an avoidable tragedy and a failure of our society to look after the people within it. I think it is our collective responsibility to educate people to have the skills to meet the challenges of life with wisdom, so that they can cope and not go under. Having the emotional skills to meet adverse circumstances with wisdom is like learning to swim, and can be imparted through education.

The effects of stress on our health make for an alarming reading, but the good news is that we can do something about it. We have assumed that we cannot do anything about problems which emerge from our inner spaces – like stress, anger, violence, and conflict in our relationships. Why is that? When faced with problems like smallpox, or cancer, or a shortage of food, or looking for new sources of energy, we are inventive and usually find a solution. We would never live with high blood pressure or diabetes and do nothing about it because we know that both can damage our health in the long-term. Why have we accepted stress as a part of life, such that it has no solution, particularly in light of the health problems it can cause? We focus on treating the symptoms of stress, but that does not offer any long-term freedom from it.

Perhaps we also need to pay attention to our modern life-style and ask if it is responsible for the epidemic of stress that we are seeing in the world right now. What can we do to change the way we live to reduce the stress in our lives? Alongside the internal changes we need to make as a result of a deeper understanding of the nature of stress, we could also consider making some external changes and the two together may help us live with a manageable amount of stress.

As we have explored in this chapter, stress can manifest as physical symptoms, it can cause mental health problems like depression, anxiety, and substance abuse, and is classified depending on how long it lasts and when it arises after a traumatic event. Stress can also affect our physical health in different ways by impacting our immune system, and can contribute to an early death, heart disease, or stroke. It also increases the risk of suicide and self-harm. For our physical and mental well-being, it is important therefore to explore the subject in some depth, to see if we can find ways of avoiding it, and deal with it in fresh ways when it does occur in our lives.

EXTERNAL CAUSES OF STRESS

WHEREVER WE MAY HAPPEN TO live in the world, and whatever our circumstances, one thing is certain – life is going to present us with challenges. We can anticipate some of these challenges, but others are unpredictable and come out of the blue. Preparing for these challenges *before* they arrive, and understanding them more deeply once they do, allows us to be ready. We can avoid them entirely in many cases, and deal with them freshly when they do inevitably befall each of us.

There are common themes which cause stress in all our lives. Money, exams, work, relationships, and health are common causes of stress. We need money to survive and having a healthy relationship with personal finances is important for us to be happy. It is not always the case that the more we have, the happier we will be. Educational systems around the world are built around teaching and testing, and this is also responsible for so much stress. Most people need to work and that can be a major cause of stress as well. There may be some things we can control within our work environments and cultures, for example, how we deal with colleagues, but others that we cannot. Having a positive and healthy attitude here can be very helpful. Almost all human beings are in a relationship with others, and given the way our minds function, these connections can be a significant cause of stress. Understanding ourselves helps us to understand others and have better relationships. Our health is something we often take for granted, but if that changes, that can be a major source of challenges also.

These are just several of the top, common sources of stress we all share. I am sure you can think of many others unique to your life and to the lives of those you care about. Below, we will also discuss other external causes of stress, like change, social media, and dealing with adverse events such as crime and failure.

So, knowing that stress is not something we can avoid, the question is: what, in the face of it all, can we do to remain healthy?

MONEY

Both, the lack of it and too much of it, can cause problems leading to stress. Dealing with poverty and the daily struggle to meet basic needs for food, shelter, clothing, education, and health is a challenge that hundreds of millions of people face daily. Once our basic needs are met, we take them for granted, and we want more – more money, better houses, holidays, clothes, electronic devices, and so on. All of these things bring pleasure, the need for which operates in the background and continues no matter how much we have. Our definition of what we regard as 'essential' in our life keeps changing to accommodate our desires, and if we do not have enough money to get what we want, that can cause stress. Arguing about money is one of the main causes of tension between couples. I have seen many relationships between couples and family members sour over money, and it often brings out our naked self-interest in ways that few other things do. How can we stop money from spoiling our relationships? It is better to talk about the issues that arise before they do because in the heat of an argument over money, all common sense flees the room and we can damage valuable relationships without thinking of the consequences.

Being able to manage money is a skill that we all need to learn. A head teacher once told me this story: her school is in a deprived area of England. She had a parent in tears one day and invited her to her office and asked why. The lady said she had no money to buy food for her child and that was really distressing her. The head teacher then sat her down with a cup of tea and went through all her income and expenditure. It turned out the lady made a lot of impulsive purchases of non-essential items whenever she passed a shop, and that added up over the month. All that was needed to solve the problem was to teach her some simple tips on money management.

We equate happiness with pleasure. Since money can buy pleasure, which makes us happy, we think it is logical that the more money we have, the happier we will be. That does not always follow, much to our disappointment. Why does having much more money than we need, sometimes lead to more stress rather than more happiness? The answer to that lies in exploring the nature of pleasure. The unconscious need for pleasure can make us buy things that we do not really need, with money we cannot always afford, for a thrill that is almost always short-lived. Once a pleasure ends it leaves a feeling of emptiness that demands to be filled. The emptiness can push us into wanting to repeat that pleasure and buy the same thing again, but this time it has to be more expensive and better. We are usually not aware of the process of pleasure operating in the background, directing our actions. I was discussing this with some school children, and the teacher in attendance piped up to say that he was the same and was into buying trainers. He already had 15 pairs, but was looking for his next one. You can imagine that a person who can buy anything he or she wants will quickly get bored of the whole thing, not be sure what to do about that, and become stressed as a result.

The need for pleasure can also drive people into gambling. It can start with small bets, and now, several online gambling websites lure people in with free money to bet with. They know that they can get you hooked very quickly. Young people are especially vulnerable and it has become a major social problem in the UK, with the Gambling Commission saying 450,000 children under 16 gamble regularly. The National Health Service in the UK is to introduce special gambling clinics to help them. If children could be taught about the nature of pleasure, not as a bad thing, but something to be understood, they would be able to avoid the problems linked to gambling.

How can we explore the subject of money with intelligence, so that it has the right place in our lives? This requires self-understanding, which can also allow us to look at money itself in new ways as well. For example, money can also be a force for good in the world, and if we can live simply, well within our means, we can also be generous and help others as needed.

CRIME

In 2017-18, 14% of UK adults reported being victims of crime. The victims, who are often among the most vulnerable in society, often do not have the resilience or skills to deal with the acute stress that follows.

How can we get over a traumatic event, make our peace with what has happened and move on, and not allow the painful memory to condition us for the rest of our lives? To start with, we have to deal with the shock of what happened, and if we can focus on the daily routine of our lives, noticing the small things like the food we eat and the trees outside, that itself can bring us into the present where there is no trauma. We can see that the pain comes from our memory, when we think about what has happened. It is not in the here and now. Ruminating over what happened reinforces the memory of that event. If we can clearly see what is happening, we can break the cycle by doing some breathing exercises, being in nature, and talking about what has happened with friends. We can also become aware of the process of conditioning, and notice how life events have an unconscious way of residing in our memory, and then influencing our thoughts and behaviour in the future. If we can be aware of that process going on, we can bring that hidden process into the light, and that allows us to respond with our intelligence. We may see what is happening and we can decide that we do not want our past to determine our future without our awareness or our consent. This allows us to move on, accept what has happened, and find peace.

When looked at from a certain point of view, the victims of crime are not just those assaulted upon. Those who choose to commit crimes were often also victims themselves, of past atrocities and/or a host of other social ills from which it can be challenging to escape, but not impossible. Leaving old patterns of behaviour and thinking behind first requires us to recognise how they unconsciously shape our lives, and realise that this has happened without our awareness or our consent. It also needs us to take ownership of our thoughts and actions, and re-examine the stories we tell ourselves, where we are often the victims. We need to stop blaming others for how we feel. That allows us the freedom to travel inwards and make the changes on the inside that can give our life a fresh direction and a new purpose.

Work

Work can cause stress in many ways; a demanding workload, too much responsibility, the uncertainty of employment, difficult employers, working conditions, challenging colleagues, lack of progression, and the repetitive nature of the work. How can we create enlightened workplaces that balance the needs of employers and employees? It is in everyone's interest to do this because a stressed workforce is not productive. To begin with, we need enlightened managers who have self-understanding and inner intelligence. This allows them to get the best out of their teams, without resorting to fear, anger, bullying, and power games, yet meeting the needs of the workplace.

It is equally important that employees bring a positive attitude to work, ignore the many small things that are not always right and focus on the things that are. That positive attitude makes for happier workplaces which are beneficial for everyone. Stress also occurs if we compare ourselves with others at work and feel bad if they are doing better than us, feel that we are in a constant state of competition with others to get ahead, or have interpersonal conflicts. So much of our life is spent at work. It is vital we find intelligent ways of being that enable workplaces to be a happy experience for everyone. Happy work places are good for employers, employees, and the bottom line. Living with self-understanding and the inner intelligence that follows makes that much easier.

Exams

Education systems around the world are based on a historical model of teach and test, to check how much knowledge you have absorbed, to rank you in comparison with others, and to prove to prospective employers that you will make a good employee with the necessary skills. This model causes extraordinary amounts of stress in everyone, from young children to their parents and to the teachers who are judged on how their pupils perform. Stress derives from the fear of failure, comparison with others, pressure from parents, and the anxiety about being judged by others. It taps into our deepest insecurities, our fears of being a nobody, and of others being better than us. So many young people self-harm or commit suicide under the pressure of exams, or if they do not get the grades they want or are expected to get.

In the 21ˢᵗ century this model is outdated and needs reforming. All the knowledge we can ever learn is on our phones and at our fingertips, so memorising it all and being able to repeat it is no longer needed, except for what we need to be able to function in society and for the job we do. Understandably, historians, geographers, and maths teachers would disagree. Exams take the fun out of learning, and as soon as the exams are over, most of the knowledge we have accumulated evaporates anyway. How much of the algebra you were taught in school do you really remember? Why are we so obsessed with ranking children in a class? Is it because our minds compare all the time, so we cannot conceive of another way of being? Or because we want the pleasure of being better than others? Do we realise how much damage it causes to the confidence and self-esteem of children who are not 'good' at studies or sports? Or is it because employers need to know who are the 'best' people to hire? Many employers are finding that the skills they need most from their employees are not taught anywhere in the current education system; how to work together with diverse people in teams, how to cope with pressure and not get stressed, how to take the initiative and think creatively, how to communicate clearly, how to be a good listener, and so on. For all these skills, you need the current education system to change to include the teaching of wisdom, emotional intelligence, communication, and relationship skills.

FACING CHANGE

Most people do not like change, and the uncertainty that follows often gives rise to anxiety and stress. Examples here may include moving, getting married, starting at a new school or college, starting a new job, or having a baby. Why might change cause stress? Perhaps it is the worry about what the future might hold or moving away from the familiar. We sometimes imagine the worst possible outcome and assume it has already occurred. How can we approach potential changes in our lives with serenity or even excitement? This needs us to understand the nature of fear and anxiety, explore the roots of it in our thinking, and ask if there is another way of seeing the same situation, and other ways to respond.

EXTERNAL EVENTS

The everyday challenges of life, often mundane, are common causes of stress. These include being late, being stuck in traffic, the car or boiler breaking down, extremes of weather, children falling ill, and so on. Other events can be more traumatic, like a major accident, losing a job or a home, or seeing the horrors of war. How can we respond to these external events in such a way that our mind remains calm and serious incidents leave no long-term scars?

RELATIONSHIPS

Human beings are not always good at relationships, and they can be a significant cause of stress. Consider the high divorce rates (between 40–50%), the conflicts we see in our interpersonal relationships and the world. We usually assume that the other person is responsible for our stress, whether it is a colleague at work, a friend, family members, a romantic partner, or wife or husband. Rarely do we think that we bear any responsibility for the conflict, and instead blame the other person. We will explore the principle causes of conflict within relationships and discover they are caused by hidden patterns of thinking that all human beings share. We can use this understanding of ourselves and how our minds work to understand others better, and this can dramatically improve all our relationships. This follows naturally once we have this depth of understanding. It is really difficult to change other people, but perhaps we can begin with ourselves, which may then lead us to ask why we want to change others in the first place.

CHILDREN

Children are such a source of joy, but there are also times when they can be a source of stress. If you have a tendency to worry, children provide plenty of reasons to do so: are they growing as they should; if they cry, is something wrong with them; how will they be when they grow up; what will the world be like for them in the future; and so on. Later, we compare them to other children in their class and worry if they are falling behind, studying hard enough, or doing enough extracurricular activities. As they become teenagers, the struggle begins between what you want them to do and how they want to be. You want to shape them as per the image you hold, which is often at an unconscious level, and they want to be someone entirely different. Without being aware of it, or understanding why, we develop expectations of our children, and when they are not met, we can get hurt. As they leave education, we worry about their careers and their choice of life partners. We want to have a say in what they do with their lives, which meets with resistance, and conflict can follow. I met a man in his seventies who had not spoken to his son or seen his grandchildren for more than 20 years. His son had joined his business and they had fallen out because the son did not like being told what to do. He had left home and they had not spoken since. As he told me the story, I felt the sorrow he did, and it had not decreased over the years. We identify with our children so completely that if anything happens to them, we feel it is happening to us, and that brings its share of joy and sorrow.

Bringing up children to be excellent human beings so that they can be well-rounded, happy, and successful in the world requires the best of us, but also our wisdom and inner intelligence. We need to evolve with them as they grow, examine the many hidden patterns of our own conditioning that may dictate what we want them to be, and nurture them so that their own inner intelligence can flower. Doing these things can help us avoid the many challenges that come with having children and allow us to enjoy the journey with them.

HEALTH

We have explored how stress can cause physical and mental health problems, but it can also be a response to physical illness. The distress that a patient feels is a combination of their disease and their emotional reaction to it. Patients can have very different emotional responses to the same problem, like back pain. I saw many patients with back pain in my career. While some could just ignore it and get on with their daily lives, others experienced much more emotional suffering and as a result, stopped working and going out, which made their problem worse. Why do people have such different emotional reactions to the same problem?

Not everyone who is ill responds by getting emotionally distressed. Some of the most cheerful people I have met are patients suffering from chronic illnesses, like rheumatoid arthritis that affects multiple joints. Those patients who remained cheerful despite their disability had some traits in common. They had a positive attitude which allowed them to overcome any psychological impact of their disability. They rarely felt sorry for themselves and were grateful for what they had and could do. All of us can emulate this.

Despite knowing the impact ill-health can have on our lives, we find it challenging to adopt a lifestyle that supports our physical and mental health. Why is that? For example, despite knowing the problems of being overweight, 39.8% of Americans were classed as obese in 2015–16. Out of the adults in the UK, 28% are obese. Obesity increases the risk of developing type 2 diabetes, heart disease, cancer, sleep apnoea, and arthritis. Why can we not eat in moderation? Despite knowing the problems caused by alcohol, smoking, and drugs, why do so many people continue to consume them in excess? It is almost as if we cannot stop ourselves. This is not to be critical of people who are overweight but to explore why this happens despite us knowing that it is not good for us. We are less in control of our lives than we think.

The answer may lie in the hidden patterns of thinking that operate from behind the curtain of our awareness, pushing us to pursue pleasure and avoid our boredom, stress, and emotional pain. There are of course other factors like: aggressive marketing; the ease of eating processed, fatty, sugar-laden food designed to make us want to repeat that pleasure often; the high cost or inaccessibility of fresh food; and the lack of skills when it comes to cooking healthy meals. Living with inner intelligence can help us navigate these challenges more easily and be able to self-regulate our food habits. Understanding the nature of conditioning and how easily and unconsciously we can be influenced by advertising and society may, for example, allow us to make more intelligent food choices.

FAILURE AND LOSS

Every doctor remembers losing his first patient. For me it was a young man who had been admitted with fractures of both his thigh bones. I was a junior doctor in training at the time. He was quite stable and chatty and I put on an IV drip, informed my senior, and thought we would just operate on him in the morning. Overnight he bled from his fractures into his thigh muscles and when we saw him in the morning his pulse was thready, and despite all our efforts, he died. I carried the pain of that with me for a long time, holding myself responsible. Surgeons also remember their failures, much more than they remember the patients who did really well. I had my share of them. Nothing in my medical training had prepared me for the shock of dealing with failure.

One thing is certain in life. We are all going to lose people and things we love and experience failure at some point. It is a natural cycle of life. The only certainty is that life is uncertain and can serve up challenges at any time. We are educated to be externally successful, but not taught how to meet failure or loss with intelligence. When such moments do arrive, we feel lost and do not know how to cope. In my medical career, there were many times where I had to inform patients who had been admitted with a backache that their MRI scan showed they had cancer. Most had less than a year left to live. Shocks like that can come at any time in our lives, and we need to ask ourselves how we are going to respond. We are all going to meet with failure, whether it is an exam, a job interview, or a driving test. What is it about failure that makes it so difficult to face? Is it the event itself or the loss of self-esteem? How can we meet these challenges with intelligence and grace, so that they do not overwhelm us? Perhaps acceptance could play a key role.

SOCIAL MEDIA

Our interaction with social media can cause considerable stress, especially if you are young and have never known life without it. I ask young people I meet why social media causes them stress. They say it makes them feel that they need to be perfect, makes them compare themselves with others, presents an ideal of what they should look and act like, and is a forum where they can feel bullied. They compare how they look with others, and one student said it made her hate her body. A young man said it made him feel left out and not popular enough, which he measured by the number of 'likes' his posts got.

Many feel the pressure to impress their peers but never feel that they achieve this, which impacts negatively on their self-esteem and self-worth. It shows them things they cannot have or people they cannot be, and that causes stress. Some think that their lives are not as exciting as others. When I asked them how social media was able to make them feel and behave in specific ways without their awareness or permission, they had no answer. Our hidden patterns of thinking allow this to happen, and by becoming aware of them, we can avoid many of the problems currently caused by social media.

BEING AROUND STRESSED PEOPLE

If you walk into a room where people are stressed, anxious, or angry, you react to this energy by becoming stressed yourself, without realising why. If you are living with someone who is angry or aggressive, their negative energy can, in turn, make you feel stressed. This is an unconscious process which is poorly understood, but our moods affect others, and vice versa.

If there is a culture of negativity in an organisation, like a school or hospital, *everyone* starts feeling negative and complaining about how bad things are. I have seen this in hospitals I have worked in. This negativity can begin with one person; equally, an individual who generates a positive outlook and sees the best in situations can make others feel upbeat and positive about the same environment. All this happens unconsciously and nobody realises that this is going on. Smart organisations need to understand this and explore how best to respond.

The challenge is, how can we respond to this fact with intelligence?

The first step is to become aware of it, and that requires sensitivity. Are we aware of the effect that our moods have on people around us? Do we realise how we become influenced by the environments we live in?

IS STRESS CAUSED
BY THE EVENT
OR OUR REACTION TO IT?

Is our stress caused by the external event or by our reaction to it? If a train is cancelled, each person on the platform reacts with a different degree of stress. Each person though thinks that their reaction is justified and the correct way to respond. Most of us do not pause to consider the many different ways in which we could respond and then make a considered judgement on the best way to do so. Why is that? Because of the close association between the triggering event and our stress reaction, it is understandable that the mind assumes that the source of the stress is 'out there' and caused by the event in question. It conflates cause with effect.

A company director whom I know worked with two secretaries who shared the same job. He said both were dedicated, hard-working, and lovely people. One of them was completely relaxed about the job, would come to work and breeze through the day. The other found the job stressful, said the phone rang all the time, that there was too much typing to do, and she never got her work completed. It was exactly the same job, but their reactions could not have been more different. Why is that? If it was the work that was the cause of the stress, then both of them should have been equally stressed by the job. The difference was in the personalities of the two people concerned. Something in the way their minds functioned was different, so one was able to respond calmly, and the other got stressed. What is behind that difference?

To answer that, we have to explore where our reactions come from, and that requires an understanding of how our mind works. The person who got stressed felt her stress was entirely justified and the only way to see the situation. It is usual to respond by blaming the job, or the individual who is stressed because they are not resilient enough, or blame ourselves for getting stressed, but that does not change the situation or how we feel. Instead, we could be curious about what it is in our thinking that makes us react in the way we do, and differently from others. That question opens the door to new discoveries about ourselves. If we can uncover the underlying cause of stress in our thinking, then our automatic reaction to a situation can change, and we can be free of the stress response that follows.

Continuing with the example above, if he tried to have a conversation with the secretary about stress, it got him nowhere. She blamed the job and was certain it was the cause of her stress. He referred to her colleague, who was not stressed at all. She thought he was 'blaming' her for her stress, that her colleague did not really care about the work, and that made her defensive and even more upset.

The main reason for our reaction to any situation is hidden from our awareness and operates in the background. All we can see is the external event that is triggering our stress. We are often sure that ours is the only way to see a situation, and get upset if someone challenges that perspective. Just as we often cannot help our reactions, others cannot help theirs, so there is little point in blaming them for the way they react. A more interesting approach is to question what is going on in our thinking when a reaction is taking place. Consider asking yourself: *why do I respond in the way I do and feel convinced that this is the only way to view my current circumstance?* This is the kind of question that opens the door to intelligence. This is a simple idea, but not easy to do. Doing so requires a quiet mind to notice the reaction as it is occurring, a depth of understanding of the entire process behind it, and then the humility to question that reaction, and explore other ways of looking at the same situation, even though our mind may be telling us that we are certainly right. We can begin with small reactions, for example, when we are reading a newspaper, or watching the news on television. Our reactions are not right or wrong, but we just need to understand the process of thinking behind them. That understanding is a step on the journey to wisdom.

Try it yourself, and see what happens.

Self-understanding is an art that can be learnt, just as one would learn to swim or play the piano and I am going to walk with you, step-by-step, to help you continue to learn that for and about yourself. It is not an intellectual process, and you do not need to be clever to learn it.

In any stressful situation, there are only two ways that stress can end. Either the situation changes or we can change our reaction to it. Most of us assume that the only way to end the stress is to change the situation, and it is common sense to try and do that. For example, if there is a pebble in my shoe, I would just stop and take it out. Some situations are easy to deal with in this way, like changing a flat tyre, for example. However, there are many other situations which are not easy or possible to change. For example, we cannot change the way other people think or behave. Many events are out of our control. How can we change how we react to these situations, so that we do not get stressed? We know that chronic stress damages our health, so avoiding it and dealing with it promptly is essential. So, what are we to do? Life keeps presenting new challenges, and we cannot predict when they will arrive. All we can do is prepare ourselves to respond with intelligence. Changing how we react to situations requires us to explore and understand where our reactions come from and the hidden patterns of thinking that contribute to them. This opens the door to enquiry.

We may find this journey strange because we may have never explored our inner spaces before, and it can feel uncomfortable. This is natural. However, we need to put that behind us and keep going. This enquiry is simple and involves observing our thoughts and feelings, and then exploring what lies behind them.

An important idea to grasp that underpins this enquiry is that though the content of our memory is unique, our minds function in the same way as in other human beings, which allows us to explore it together. You may be a Christian, and another person may be Jewish, but the nature of belief is the same in both of you, or you may want a new kitchen, and your partner may want a new car, but the quality of desire is the same.

When I was speaking in different institutions about the benefits of wisdom and self-understanding, people would often come up to me and say, "Why do I need to look at and understand myself? Why can someone not just tell me what to do? I am looking for an easy solution to my stress". This approach does not usually bring lasting change. You may feel better in the short-term and get over your current stress, but the same trigger will generate the same stress reaction the next time. Trying to live our lives according to what others have said, even if the advice is hundreds of years old, usually does not work. As evidence, look at the state of humanity today despite thousands of years of teachings and words written in books which we have tried to follow. There may be some change on the surface, but deep down, we remain the same. You may read of ten tips to deal with stress and try to apply them to your life, and that can be helpful, but the underlying patterns of thinking that generate stress continue. When it comes to our inner spaces, it is the discoveries we make about ourselves and how our minds work that can bring lasting change. No one can give you this understanding. You have to take the journey inwards and find out for yourself. I believe every person is capable of this understanding, whether you are educated or not.

It is crucial to appreciate the difference between knowledge and understanding. Knowledge can be shared between people; how to change a light bulb, how to cook rice or fly a plane. Understanding comes from our own exploration and discovery. It is the difference between reading a travel book and going there yourself. Consider another analogy. I cannot tell you what water tastes like. No description can convey that. You have to drink it to find out. I can tell you that the taste of water is amazing and it is life-nourishing, and point you to the source and how to get there, but you have to do your bit to walk there yourself and drink it to discover its beauty. You could memorise and repeat everything in this book, but unless you begin your own journey of enquiry into your inner spaces, there will be no lasting change. Think of this book as a guide or a road map, but you have to do the travelling yourself. In any journey, the first step is the most important. Once you begin this inner journey of enquiry, each discovery leads to another one, and before you know it, you find that you have changed. I am going to walk you through it.

THE ART OF UNDERSTANDING OURSELVES

When an astronomer looks at the universe, it is the quality of the telescope he or she has that will determine what is discovered. When a scientist studies the structure of the cell, it is the quality of the microscope that determines what is seen. When we look at ourselves, we have no telescope or microscope, only our own powers of observation and intelligence to ask the questions that can open the door to new discoveries about ourselves. *How* we look at ourselves is the key to the discoveries we will make and to unlocking the mystery and beauty that lie within. This is the art of enquiry; how to look at our inner spaces and understand ourselves clearly, as well as the challenges and pitfalls we may encounter on this journey inwards.

This understanding is an art because it has several nuances which become apparent the more one practices it. It requires us to learn a basic set of skills of enquiry, but it is in applying them that the learning continues, and we begin to discover so much more. It becomes a life-long journey of learning without end. It is the same whether we are learning to paint, play the piano, or this art of learning how to look at and examine our inner spaces. It is rooted in the scientific method. One starts as a sceptic, doubting and questioning what we see, not believing what others (including this author) have written or said until we have seen it for ourselves. The scientific method also requires that we travel with an open mind, not rejecting something just because it feels new. I have been doing this for around 40 years and I am still learning and discovering nuances to my own self-enquiry. There is no end point to this journey, and it has been enriching from the day I began, as a young medical student.

Of all the chapters in the book, this is perhaps the most important. If you learn how to look at yourself, then you can begin your journey of self-understanding, and will make your own discoveries along the way. I share here what I have learnt thus far in the hope that it may be a stepping stone to your own.

HOW DO WE BEGIN?

How do we begin to look at ourselves? When I tried to explain this to my mother, she used to say, "I know how to look at myself in the mirror, but I do not know how to look at my thoughts and feelings". How do we begin? We have never been taught how to do this.

It is quite simple. An easy way to begin is to use a conversation. Just notice how the other person interrupts you as you are speaking. That act of paying attention is awareness. Now observe what is happening in your thinking as the conversation proceeds. Notice the thoughts and feelings that arise in your mind and when you start thinking about what you are going to say next. As you do so, notice that you are now only half-listening to the other person speak because you are waiting for your cue to say what you need to. Observe your urge to say something and when it arises. Notice as well if you interrupt the other person to say it (vs. waiting for them to complete their thought). This simple act of paying attention and noticing our thoughts and feelings as they arise, is self-awareness.

Now ask yourself two questions and see what emerges. *Why do I have this urge to speak rather than listen? What does this conversation reveal about how my mind works?* You may discover that your mind is reactive, instantly responding to what is said. You may also discover that we all have an urge to express ourselves. Talking about ourselves makes us feel good. Listening does not bring the same pleasure, so we do not do that as well. Noticing these distinctions can bring greater self-understanding. If you go further, you will realise that this is the same in all human beings. Understanding yourself helps you to understand others better.

PASSION

We need energy to thrive in the world, to study, work, have relation-ships, and keep physically fit. We also need energy to explore our inner spaces. Without this energy or passion, we cannot go far. If we want to do something and consider it to be important, we will find the energy for it. If we have an exam tomorrow, we will have the energy to sit and study for long hours. If we are in love, we find the energy to make time for the other person. If we want to run a marathon, we find the energy to train for it.

What might inspire me to develop a passion for this enquiry into my inner spaces?

As I observe my life, I see the conflict in my relationships and ask if it is possible to live in harmony with myself, with others, and the earth. That question becomes a passion. As I observe the stress I feel in my dealings with the world, I ask myself if it is possible to live a life without long-term stress, which I know can damage my health. That question gives me the energy to find out. I see the awful state of the world – its inequality, brutality, loss of entire species, and the rising spectre of global warming – and ask why humanity is where it is. Despite our so-called intelligence and capability, why are we destroying the planet we call home and robbing future generations of the resources they will need to survive? I can see that all these problems have their origin in the way the human mind works, and trying to understand what is going on gives me great passion. I know that I have only one life to live, and it could end at any time. I want to live it without conflict, with a sense of peace, be happy, and make intelligent choices in my life. I want to do something I love doing and meet life's challenges with serenity, without getting stressed. I know that for all this I need a different kind of intelligence, and that comes naturally from understanding myself and how my mind works. This gives me the energy to begin. You will have to find your own reasons why this enquiry is important and urgent. This will give you the passion that you need for this inner journey.

If we are serious about this enquiry, we also need to give it time and create space in our mind to explore these questions. We waste so much of our energy: in conflict, keeping busy, on our phones, and endless entertainment. By creating space, I mean that we need a mind that is not always preoccupied and buzzing with thoughts. This could mean we are still from time to time, and will perhaps write in our journal, or go for a walk in nature on our own. If we want to learn the guitar, we could buy one in our initial enthusiasm, but if we make no time and space to learn and practise, it is just going to gather dust. Once we have mastered the art of looking at ourselves, we carry that awareness with us throughout the day, and it becomes second nature.

A SPIRIT OF LEARNING

It is worth embracing a spirit of learning to embark on this journey, to learn about ourselves and how our minds work. This is not easy because as we get older, our minds become full of so many certainties. We think we know everything about ourselves and the world. A spirit of learning implies we begin with humility, with a sense of not knowing, keen to learn and uncover the hidden ways in which our minds work. On this inner journey, our mind needs to remain open to discovering the new, and it cannot do so if it is attached to the old. You may come across something new that challenges your existing certainties. In response, an internal reaction can arise, which is critical or dismissive. That is a natural reaction, and not right or wrong. Is it possible for us to observe that reaction, put it to one side, and keep exploring? We need a mind that neither rejects something because it is new or different, nor accepts anything blindly, without question. Since we are exploring the mind that we all share, what you read is only true if you see that clearly for yourself.

How does our mind receive information? We can observe that often our mind takes in what it already knows and agrees with, and either ignores or is critical of the rest. Along with a university lecturer, I once hosted a session exploring stress with students. At the end of the session, we asked them to discuss and provide feedback on what they had learnt. To our surprise, the discussion and feedback reflected what they already knew, rather than anything new we had shared with them. All our minds function in similar ways. If we want a mind that is open to learning, we need to be aware of this process going on in the background.

Education should be all about *learning*; instead, it has become mostly about *teaching*. The teacher transfers the knowledge from his or her mind to the student. This is the accepted model of education worldwide. The student receives it, memorises it, and repeats it in an exam. This is, of course, important in some ways, but as a result, our education has not prepared us for learning. As adults, we have lost the natural curiosity that two-year olds have about the world around them. We want someone to tell us what to do, and then we can apply it to our lives. This may work in the world outside, but does not work as well when we explore the world within.

In exploring our inner spaces, knowledge, like this book, can serve as a guide, but we need to take that journey ourselves, and for that, we need this spirit of learning. A guidebook about London is a poor substitute to seeing the city yourself, though it can make your trip much richer and more informed.

It is a journey without a destination because there is no end to learning, whether it is about music, or ourselves. I have met people who have been reading different books and trying to apply that knowledge to their lives for many years, but feel that they are no further forward. What you learn, and the way that impacts your life, depends on the quality of the enquiry, and the passion, curiosity, and sensitivity you bring to it. Learning is in the moment and continues life-long.

OUR MINDS FUNCTION IN SIMILAR WAYS

We human beings think that we are unique because we look different, speak different languages, and have many cultural differences. We have all had different experiences, which are stored in our memory. We identify with those memories as the 'me'. Our memories shape our personalities, and that reinforces our sense of being separate, unique.

Hidden from our awareness, however, just as our hearts function in similar ways, our minds do as well. We cannot see the way the heart functions, and the same is true of our mind. Understanding the way our heart works allowed scientists to prevent and solve many problems linked to the heart, including drugs for blood pressure and heart failure, stents for blocked arteries, and defibrillators. Understanding the way our minds works can also help us avoid and treat the many problems that emerge from our thinking, like stress.

The feeling of stress that we all experience is the same as are the mechanisms behind it, though the severity of it and the causes may be unique to each of us. The nature of pleasure, desire, fear, and anger are the same in all of us as well, allowing us to explore them together. We all have the same emotional requirements: to be happy, loved, listened to, and understood.

Consider another analogy. Different computers have unique content stored in their hard drives but may share the same operating system, which is hidden from the user. This operating system controls how the computer works. Similarly, our minds have unique memories stored in the brain, but hidden from our awareness, they work in the same way in all humans. This makes it easier for us to accept ourselves as we are. As we will explore, this is an important step in our journey of enquiry.

EXPLORING FROM THE PARTICULAR TO THE GENERAL

This is a very important idea to grasp, so please take your time and walk with me as we explore it.

If I am afraid of losing my job, for example, exploring from the particular to the general means instead of spending all my time feeling anxious about my job, I go deeper and explore the nature of fear itself. In that journey, I may have an insight and realise, for example, that some fears are not real, but just a product of my imagination. Other fears are inevitable (like dying), and just need to be accepted. In doing so, my fear of losing my job may end, allowing me to respond with intelligence. I could begin looking for a new job, just in case. Not only would this insight help me get over my fear of losing my job, but also apply to all fears that I may encounter in the future.

When we think of a stressful situation, we focus on what caused our stress, how it affected us, our reaction to it, our opinion about the other person, and so on. All this comes from the content of our particular memory and is about 'me'. We think that the problem and our reaction to it are unique to us. We may go to see a psychologist or counsellor and talk things over. This may make us feel better, but does not illuminate the root of the problem, and may not prevent the stress from recurring. An alternative approach is to go from thinking about the causes of my stress to exploring the nature of stress itself. We can do this by asking questions.

It is in exploring the hidden patterns of thinking that generate our stress that we can be genuinely free, and that requires us to go from thinking about the particular cause of our stress to exploring the nature of stress itself.

SENSITIVITY

To notice our thoughts and feelings as they arise in us, the first quality we need is sensitivity. This is a skill that we can nurture and develop. Children have this naturally, but we seem to lose it as we get older. Without that, we cannot begin. Some thoughts and feelings are quiet, subtle, and in the background. We need an extraordinary sensitivity to notice them. If we are to learn about ourselves, the first step is to notice what is happening.

This sensitivity is different from 'being too sensitive', which refers to taking things to heart. Here I am using the word sensitive in terms of our ability to notice things.

We use our senses to notice the world around us; the song of an unseen blackbird, the quiet murmur of a stream, or the smell of a jasmine bush in the garden. We use our senses to feel the coolness of the trunk of a eucalyptus tree and the subtle taste of cardamom in a curry dish. We also use them to notice others – what they are thinking or feeling. We may see that someone is quieter than normal, and ask why. The more sensitive we are, the more we will perceive in the world around us. When we turn our gaze inwards, the same quality of sensitivity allows us to notice our thoughts and feelings. It is easier to notice the big emotions like anger and fear. It is more difficult to discern the feeling of envy as it arises in us when we see someone in a fancy car and the process of comparison behind it.

How can we nurture this sensitivity? Perhaps we could begin by finding out what causes the mind to become insensitive. We cannot be sensitive to our thoughts and feelings if we are being bombarded by external stimuli. Examples of this include our time spent browsing the internet, television, reading, and other forms of entertainment. We also lose our sensitivity if we have a mind that is busy from morning till night – either working or gathering new experiences. A mind in conflict obviously cannot be sensitive. Stress affects up to 80% of people in some surveys and is an obvious barrier to sensitivity. A mind that is on fire cannot notice what is going on in the world around, or within.

Can this sensitivity be nurtured? Nature is a great teacher and spending time in it is a good start. We could begin by sitting in a garden and notice how many birds we can hear, for example. We can nurture sensitivity in children by asking them to notice what they can see in a patch of grass or to notice different smells. Making some time to be quiet can enhance the sensitivity of the brain. This is challenging because our daily life feels busy. Our mind wants to be occupied and stimulated and resists being quiet and doing nothing. We can make time to be quiet in the middle of a busy day, even for ten minutes, just sitting quietly, noticing our breathing. You do not have to give this quietness a name or follow any system. As our mind becomes more sensitive to the world around it, the same sensitivity then carries over to observe the thoughts and feelings in our inner spaces.

Try this. Sit still somewhere and write down every thought that arises during that time. You are not aiming for a quiet mind, just noticing each thought as it comes and goes. Notice the obvious ones, but then also the subtle, fleeting ones. Gradually you become aware of the quieter, more fleeting thoughts and feelings. That is sensitivity.

COMMITMENT

You need a commitment to learn anything new – a new language or a musical instrument. Wanting to learn something gets us started, but it is our commitment that gets us through. So many people begin to learn a musical instrument, for example, but give up because it is difficult and they do not get the benefits quickly enough. Those who stick with it enjoy playing for a lifetime. This journey into our inner spaces to understand ourselves is no different. When you begin, you have to accept that there will be times when it feels hard, and the benefits you wanted from it may not come quickly enough. When that happens, you have to commit yourself to keep going. The benefits of learning a new language or a musical instrument are tangible. They can be seen in others, but the benefits of this enquiry are intangible, and you have to discover them for yourself.

How can we nurture this commitment to self-enquiry? Having a friend who you can discuss things with is very helpful, as is keeping a journal. You could set up an enquiry group in your area, and meeting people with a shared interest in this enquiry can renew our commitment to ourselves.

I first began asking questions about life more than 40 years ago. My enthusiasm and curiosity have not dimmed over that period. I have found that the enquiry has nourished me. Each question I explore unpeels another layer of the onion and leads to a new discovery. I did not 'decide' that I was going to stick with it for this long. It just happened, and it has transformed my life in innumerable ways.

CURIOSITY

Human beings are curious by nature. All the discoveries we have made in the world began with a particular curiosity. Isaac Newton watched an apple fall from a tree, asked why, and discovered gravity. We spend a lot of money on research to fund this curiosity that we have about the world around us. The National Cancer Institute in America has an annual budget of over $6 billion for cancer research. On the other hand, we have almost completely neglected the world within and the same curiosity does not extend to our inner spaces. Why is that? Why have we just accepted that there is no answer to human stress, anxiety, violence, loneliness, and fear? Our unconscious habits lead to smoking and obesity, which contribute to many cancers. Why have we just accepted these habits as inevitable?

How can we nurture this curiosity in ourselves? Nature can be a great teacher. As we walk through a wood, we could be curious about what we see and want to find out more. This curiosity led ecologist Suzanne Simard to discover that trees communicate with each other and send each other nutrients using a network of fungal filaments in the ground. Someone's curiosity led to a discovery that has enriched human understanding.

Can we begin by being curious about where our thoughts and feelings come from, and uncover the many hidden patterns of thinking that make us who we are? This curiosity has no goal. Its reward is the joy of discovering something new about ourselves. You could make a discovery that may benefit all of humanity. The intelligent mind is always curious and open to learning about itself.

QUESTIONS ARE IMPORTANT

Asking questions of the life that we live is the key to unlocking the door to discoveries about ourselves and how our minds work. Questions open the door to curiosity and get us started on journeys of exploration. We need to expand our horizons and ask questions that we usually would not ask. Since we share the same mind with other human beings, we can question it together. Instead of looking at the stars together and sharing what we learn, we can look at our inner spaces and do the same. These are some of the questions that I am exploring at present, but you will have your own:

- Where do my opinions come from, and why am I attached to them?
- Why does my mind automatically compare itself to others? What are the implications of that? What would happen if it did not do so?
- What is behind my feeling of stress? Does it lie in my thinking?
- Why is there so much conflict in human relationships, and so much unhappiness?
- Why is there such an inherent lack of kindness in human beings?
- Why do we want to be happy? Is it because we are not happy now?

When we are asked a question, we look into our memory for an answer. Or, we look to see what others have said. To explore and understand ourselves, we need a different approach because the answers do not reside in our memory. This understanding does not come from our memory, but from seeing something freshly in the present moment. A fact discovered freshly in the moment has the power to transform, whereas an idea that comes from my memory, or someone else's, does not. You will notice that not all questions have easy answers. That is okay. It is essential to ask and hold the questions anyway because a more profound understanding can emerge freshly, from the question itself.

The first question when exploring any subject could be, "What questions can we ask to understand this better?" For example, if I say, "I am terrified of spiders", and I want to understand the root of that, there are three lines of enquiry that open up:

- Questions about spiders, how many are poisonous, what precautions I can take, etc. Studying the object of my fear in detail may make me realise that my fears are unfounded.
- Questions about the nature of fear itself. What is the nature of fear? Where does it originate? Is it the same in all human beings? What are my unconscious fears? What is the process of thinking that gives rise to fear? Are my fears rational? How many of them come to pass?
- Questions about the 'I' that feels the fear. Who am I? How is this 'I' put together? If I try to look for it in myself, why can I not find it? Is it constant, or always changing?

Questions can sometimes be quite challenging. For example, if someone asks me, "Do you always act from your self-interest?", I may react with anger, get upset, and ask an equally sharp question back. If I am open to learning, I will watch and learn from my reaction as well.

If we are willing to explore them, our reactions are a great learning opportunity. In the example above, I could ask, "Why did I react negatively to that question and what does it reveal about me?" I may discover that I have an image of myself as someone who is not selfish and react when that is challenged. I could then ask, "Am I selfish? Does my self-interest operate in quiet ways behind the scenes? How does it influence my behaviour?" I may discover that all human beings act from self-interest, and are aware of it only to varying degrees. I could then ask, "How can two people who are acting from their hidden self-interest, have a happy and harmonious relationship?", and so on. What started as a reaction becomes a starting point to learning more about myself and how my mind works, and this may allow me to understand and accept others better, and live with intelligence.

No right or wrong

This is a key concept to grasp, and one that may feel counter-intuitive. Many people find this an obstacle to continuing with their enquiry.

We are constantly passing judgement on the world around us and on our thoughts and feelings. We label feelings as being good or bad, or right or wrong. This comes from our conditioning, which we will explore later. Judging ourselves and others is an unconscious and automatic process. We either justify what we are thinking or feeling as right, or are critical of ourselves for what we feel. Both are a barrier to curiosity and enquiry. Why?

If I think jealousy is 'wrong', then I cannot look at it, and immediately try and not be jealous. If I think it is justified, I do not bother to look at it either. If I think being selfish is 'bad', then I try hard to be 'selfless' and may even convince myself that my charitable works are proof of that. All that happens is that my so-called 'selfishness' just gets buried, and continues to act from behind the screen of my awareness because it is not understood.

If everyone in society around me is saying 'racism' is a terrible thing, then I just bury all my opinions and dislikes of minorities and pretend that I am accepting of them. I may make a token gesture to show that I am not a racist because I hate that label. Deep down, however, and probably hidden from my awareness, nothing changes, and my prejudices bubble up and express themselves when I am off-guard and least expecting it.

If I can accept whatever emerges from my inner spaces and ask, "Why do I think or feel this way?", then the doorway to intelligence opens, and I can walk through it.

How can I accept myself as I am when I know that so many things I feel are 'wrong'? Are envy, hatred, selfishness, and racism not wrong? The idea that things are right and wrong come from our unconscious conditioning. They serve a useful purpose to help us live in an orderly society but can be a hindrance to self-acceptance and learning.

Without this acceptance, there can be no curiosity and learning about ourselves. If I do not accept that I have prejudices, then I cannot begin to enquire into what lies behind them. Moreover, I know that the human mind functions in similar ways in all human beings, so the emotions I feel are not unique to me. I just think I am the only one feeling stressed or anxious or jealous, but I am not. This realisation aids the acceptance of myself as I am, which in turn allows my enquiry to proceed.

In the same way, other people cannot help the emotions they feel. Those emotions come from their conditioning influences, which they are not aware of, just like me. This understanding can result in compassion. We are all, of course, accountable for our actions, and there is no getting away from that.

THREE STEPS TO SELF-ENQUIRY

Though it is one unified process, for simplicity, I suggest that there are three simple steps to begin to learn about ourselves and how our mind works. None of these three steps come intuitively to us because this approach was not part of our education. They will feel a bit strange at first, but become second nature as you travel. Let us walk through this together.

The first step is to observe what is happening in our inner spaces, to notice our thoughts and feelings as they arise in us. As we have explored, this needs sensitivity, curiosity, and passion.

The second step is to accept what we find without judging it as good or bad, or right or wrong, because that can block our enquiry. Taking ownership of our feelings is counter-intuitive because it appears to us that they are somebody's fault. As we have discussed, this is important, but not easy.

The third step is to ask why we think or feel that way. For example, in exploring envy, we may discover that the mind compares itself with others all the time, and then explore why that is. It is this third step that awakens our inner intelligence.

Let me illustrate this with an example. Suppose I am a Christian (I am not), and you are critical of my religion. I feel challenged and upset.

I retaliate by saying unflattering things about your religion and defend my own, and an argument begins. How can I learn from this, use my intelligence to explore what is happening, and diffuse the conflict? The first step is to notice that I am angry and upset. The second step is to accept that my emotional attachment to my religion is behind my anger. The nature of all attachment is that I want to defend what I am attached to. This is not right or wrong, just a fact. The third step is to question why I feel hurt. That leads me to explore the nature of belief. *Why am I attached to my beliefs? Where do they come from? Which of my emotional needs do they meet? Is the same process at work in the other person?* These questions open the door to intelligence and result in freedom from all conflict linked to belief. I realise that though I am a Christian and you have a different religion, the nature of faith is the same in both of us, and we are the same human being, despite our superficial differences. The conflict between us ends immediately.

This concept of attachment, and identification, is endemic to the human experience. Many religions, for example, refer to *attachment* as being one of the causes of human sorrow, and therefore advocate 'detachment' as a way of overcoming it. This does not work because the mind that is attached is also the mind that says, "I should be detached", and gets frustrated when it cannot do so. A different approach is to explore why the mind gets attached to its opinions, beliefs, possessions, people, and so on, in the first place. Our minds get attached to anything which meets our deep-seated emotional needs. If we want to live with detachment, we have to begin by understanding those needs and exploring where they come from. If we can find their source, and our hearts are full, and we live with a sense of peace, our inner needs drop away and so do all our attachments.

This simple three-step approach of looking, accepting, and questioning, allows us to see past those attachments, explore our entire emotional landscape, and learn as we travel.

THE THREE STAGES OF INSIGHT

Insight results in a fundamental change and is the process by which something within us is seen clearly, like a ray of sunlight on a lake on a cloudy day. It does not involve logic and does not come through thinking things through. It is not linked to memory. It is not a thing of the past. It is fresh, and in the present, like a flash of lightning that cannot be repeated even if we want to.

For example, if we are on the same course in college, and you are telling me about how well you have done in your exams, I start feeling bad. Insight is seeing clearly that I am envious because my mind is comparing itself with others all the time, in the background. I ask why that is, and how I can respond with intelligence to that fact. I notice that process at work in other areas of my life. How can I respond with intelligence to this fact? Once that unconscious process of thinking is seen clearly, which is an insight, I cannot go back. That insight changes me. Every time the feeling of envy arises in me, I see the process of comparison behind it, and it stops immediately. Over time, the feeling of envy does not arise at all.

For the sake of simplicity, we could break this process of insight into three stages, though it is a unitary process.

We know the mind reacts quickly to events, and in the example above, I would start feeling bad as you are talking to me and not understand why. I would blame you for making me feel bad.

The first stage of insight is to look back at what has already happened. I understand I felt bad because of envy, realise the process of comparison behind it, and ask how I can meet it with intelligence.

The second stage of insight is to be aware of the feeling of envy as it arises in me. At that moment, I am also aware of the process of comparison behind it. This happens in real-time. As it does so, there is a realisation that this process of comparison is an automatic, but not an intelligent response, and the feeling of jealousy melts away. There is no effort required in this process, and I am not trying to suppress the feeling. Suppressing a feeling without understanding it just buries it, and it bubbles away underneath until it finds another occasion to express itself, getting stronger each time.

The third stage of insight is when the reaction does not occur at all. In watching my responses, and meeting them with intelligence each time, something shifts inside me. When you are telling me about your amazing achievement, there are no feelings of comparison and envy at all, and I can be simply happy for you.

On this journey of enquiry, insight can come at any time, and it is incredible when it does. It is like seeing the beauty of a sunrise for the first time, and it dispels the darkness. It brings clarity and leaves us changed. I can share a personal example. Whenever I was criticised, even over simple things like leaving lights on in the house, I used to become defensive, get upset and react negatively, blaming the other person for hurting my feelings. I would find something critical to say about them and sometimes harbour a resentment against them. I was curious and began to explore what was going on inside me when faced with criticism. Why was it so hurtful? I had an insight into the fact that I carried with me many unconscious images or opinions of myself, and I felt hurt when they were challenged. I realised that criticism was a chance for learning and improvement. This insight has changed my reaction to criticism. Now I do not react in the old way, appreciate the feedback, reflect on it, and make changes, if necessary. It has transformed my relationships.

FACT VS. OPINION

When we react to a situation, it is important to ask what is the fact, and separate that from our opinion about the fact. When listening to you tell me about your new car, I may be feeling envious. The fact is that I am envious. My opinion about the fact may be that envy is only human, or that it is a sin, or it is not my fault for feeling that way, or that it is your fault for telling me your story and making me feel bad. In the shower of thoughts and feelings that arise as a reaction to an event, it is difficult to separate the fact from our opinion about the fact. If I ask myself, "What is the fact here?", then it becomes clear.

Focusing on the fact allows us to delve into it further, and find out what is behind it. The fact could be that I am selfish, or that I am unkind, or have an image of myself that is not true, or feel empty and lonely inside. Our opinions about the fact may be different from others, but the core facts of the way our minds work are the same in all of us, allowing us to come together and explore them.

Try this. Next time you are stressed, write down these questions and see what emerges:

- What am I feeling?
- What is the fact?
- What is my opinion about the fact?
- What questions can I ask to explore the fact further?

ACCEPTING RESPONSIBILITY

Accepting responsibility for the feelings that arise within us is one of the keys to this enquiry. If we are stressed, for example, then accepting that the stress originates in our thinking is not easy. We find it challenging to take responsibility for our feelings, and our first instinct is to blame ourselves or others. Blaming others makes it more difficult for us to understand why we reacted in the way we did. If a friend does not contact me to congratulate me on my promotion, we think it is his or her fault for hurting us. Accepting responsibility allows us to ask why we feel that way, and in exploring that, we may discover that it is our own unmet expectation that is causing our pain. This leads us to ask where our expectations come from and if they are our responsibility or somebody else's. Accepting responsibility for how we feel enables us to learn about ourselves. Blaming others denies us that chance of learning.

This does not absolve people for their behaviour towards us but allows us to learn from our reactions to them.

Because our mind thinks in terms of "whose fault is this?" or "what is 'right or wrong'?", it is difficult for us to take ownership of how we feel. Our feeling hurt has to be somebody's fault – either ours or the other person's. If we can leave behind notions of right and wrong, we can explore what is actually going on in our thinking. That leads to illumination.

Rather than focusing on whose fault it is, I can be curious as to the origin of the feeling of stress because it has arisen in my mind. Why did I get stressed? What can I learn about myself from my stress reaction? This enquiry allows us to explore the only thing in our control, which is our reaction. If we can change that, our stress can dissolve.

KNOWLEDGE VS. UNDERSTANDING

I have touched on this before but will expand on it further here because it is so important. There is a subtle but important distinction between the two, especially in the context of self-enquiry. It can determine whether this understanding illuminates and transforms our life or leaves us frustrated because we feel we have not changed.

You may read in a book, for example, that envy is caused by the mind comparing itself with others all the time. You may listen to that, and store that in your memory, and be able to repeat it and convince yourself that it is something you now *know* as a fact. All that has happened, though, is that the fact has gone from the book to your memory. You will find that despite being able to repeat that fact, nothing in your life changes and you are still as envious as before. You may get frustrated that you have not changed, despite 'knowing' it all. You may read this book, and be able to repeat it, and become an expert on it, but that knowledge may not bring change. You will still get envious and stressed and then be critical of the book or its author.

Understanding something deeply has a completely different impact.

The key difference is that you actually observe the feeling of envy unfold in your thinking, watch it carefully, and enquire yourself into its origins, and what is behind it. You do it each time it arises in you – not *applying* what you know, but observing it freshly. As you do so, a mysterious process begins, and you will realise one day that the envy has completely gone and you cannot figure out why. It is mysterious, perhaps, because we do not notice it happening, and that is because it probably does not involve thinking.

This idea becomes particularly relevant if you are trying to pass this understanding on to others, say to a group of students. You need to awaken this understanding in them by asking questions about the mind we all share and then exploring those questions with them in an open way. Just telling them ten facts that they need to memorise and apply in their life will have little long-term impact.

A realisation that we come to, through our own enquiry, has the potential to bring transformation.

LOOKING WITHOUT LANGUAGE

As we look at the world, our mind continually names what it sees, in order to make sense of what is happening. We name our emotions in the same way. Our mind also edits out a huge amount of the stimuli it receives. This is an essential function of the mind.

Try this little experiment. Look at a rose or a picture of any other flower you know, and notice what happens in your mind as you do so. Most of the time, we name it as a rose and stop looking any further.

Now try looking at the same flower, but this time without a single thought coming in the way of that observation. Did you find that you noticed so much more about the same flower, the intricate play of shadows, light, and beauty? Did you find that as you kept looking and noticing the details of the flower, your mind became quieter?

The same process applies to our feelings. When we name a feeling, we stop observing it, and then respond *to the name we have given it.* That name triggers all the associations with it from our memory. Continuing with our example of envy, if it arises in me as you are telling me about your fabulous new home, and I name it as envy, then that word triggers a shower of responses from my memory. The responses repeat the same pattern of thoughts that have been triggered before. These may justify the feeling, think it is only human, or be critical of me, or you. Or, I may feel guilty about feeling envious, think I am a bad person, and beat myself up over that. I lose touch with the original feeling that arose as I heard your story, and just as with the rose, my chance to learn more about it fades away. If, on the other hand, I can observe it as it arises in me, without naming it, my mind becomes quiet, and I can learn so much more about it.

How can I observe a feeling without naming it when my mind is so used to naming everything? Again, nature is a great teacher. Observe a sunset and notice how initially you just look at it and your mind wanders off to think of other things. Now go back to it, and this time watch it without a single thought coming in the way. Keep watching in this way as long as you can. Notice as you do so how your mind becomes quiet. If we can do this with a sunset, we can also do this with our feelings as they arise in us. It is simple, but not easy. Try it and find out. It is a beautiful skill to learn.

Though language is essential for communication, it is not essential for observing something clearly, whether it is a thinking process, a feeling, or a tree. The moments of clarity and insight we have, which result in change, come when we observe and understand something in ourselves directly, without language coming in the way. It is an 'Aha!' moment. When I am able to see things in this way, the normal chatter of my thoughts ebbs away, and my mind becomes quiet. In that quietness, I can see things clearly, both inside and outside myself, and it feels like a sense of grace.

You may have never considered this idea before so it may feel strange. Please do not dismiss it out of hand, and explore it for yourself. Of all the ideas in this book, this one is perhaps one of the most important to grasp. It leads to insight. If you can learn this skill, of looking without language, so many amazing discoveries await.

The process of looking without language, by observing what arises in us without naming it, bypasses the normal patterns of thinking and enables insight, resulting in change, often without effort. I think it is a mysterious process because we cannot see how the change occurs. Again, it is simple, but not easy.

UNDERSTANDING THE FACT BRINGS TRANSFORMATION

If we want to climb a mountain, we start with the idea and then make an effort to do so. It is a simple process. It is natural for us to think that for inner change, we need to do the same. Suppose I see that I am selfish. I then have an idea that I want to be selfless. I practise being selfless and think that should bring about lasting change. We quickly realise that it does not work that way, and using effort to bring about a transformation in our inner spaces has only limited success. Any change is short-lived and lasts only as long as our will power is active. We get frustrated when we realise that despite all our efforts, we have not changed. Why is that?

Perhaps it is because we have two competing thought processes in our mind. One says, "I want to be selfless". The other is our self-interest, which is also a product of our thinking and which continues operating behind the boundaries of our awareness.

Change does not come from pursuing the ideal, but from exploring the fact, in this case, our abiding self-interest.

Suppose I realise I am an angry person. I think I can solve this problem by trying not to be angry, by pursuing an ideal. This works as long as my willpower is working, and even then, not so well. I get frustrated because I have not achieved what I set out to do and think of myself as having failed. The anger continues because the roots of it in my thinking have not changed. Instead, if I let go of the ideal, and focus my energy on understanding what is going on in my mind when I get angry, I discover that before my anger erupts there is a sense of being hurt, or indignation at seeing something I do not like. I decide to explore that further, and ask why I get hurt, and as I keep going, I realise that I have changed.

Similarly, it is in exploring loneliness that we can discover solitude, in exploring fear that we can get over anxiety, in understanding how our minds compare all the time that we can overcome envy, in exploring the nature of pleasure that we can overcome addiction, in exploring our emotional needs that we can stop getting hurt in relationships, and finally, in exploring the roots of stress in our thinking that we can be free of it.

When I first came to the UK, I brought with me all my conditioning and many layers of identity. I was an Indian and a Hindu. If I met someone who said something negative about India or Hinduism, I would find myself getting upset and defensive because I felt personally attacked. I began to explore what was going on and explore the nature of identity and belief. One morning I woke up and found that all my many layers of identity had disappeared, and they have never come back. I no longer felt Indian or Hindu, but just a human being. The change had occurred not through effort, but just by observing, enquiring, and understanding the nature of identity and belief.

There was a time when I was wasting time on my phone for several hours a day. I would go to check the weather perhaps, and still be there an hour later, looking at something entirely different. Any attempts I made to regulate that would last a few days, and then I would be back in the old habit. My willpower was just not enough to break a well-established habit. This is true of all habits, whether it is smoking, or eating for comfort, or drinking, and so on.

I changed my approach and decided to find out what was behind the habit I had. I realised that just before I picked up the phone, there was the flash of a thought to check something out or a feeling of restlessness. The phone provided a welcome distraction, and I could be absorbed in it for hours. I became aware that it met my need to be occupied, not feel lonely, be stimulated, and entertained. I slowed the entire process down, observing without language the thoughts and feelings that prompted me to pick up the phone. I stayed with that feeling, and it transformed into quietness. I did not resist it or give in to it, but just stayed with it. Since that feeling of restlessness was not there any longer, the need to constantly be occupied on the phone also went away. As I got better at noticing and being with that feeling, my phone usage decreased, and the habit was broken.

The change occurred not because of my willpower, but through enquiry and a deeper understanding of the patterns of thinking that were behind the habit. I was not trying to change anything, but just observing what was actually happening. The deeper I was able to go behind the scenes, noticing the hidden processes behind my habits, the more I seemed to change.

These habits creep up on us quietly, and suddenly they feel too strong to break. This approach is simple, but not easy. It requires us to put into practice all the things we will have learnt throughout this book. It depends on the sensitivity, passion, and commitment that we bring to the enquiry, and the ability to notice thoughts and feelings without language.

Hidden expectations

On any journey, we have expectations that we hope it will fulfil. We judge its success based on how many of our expectations are met. This applies equally to a new relationship, a new job, as well as this journey of self-enquiry. Some expectations may be obvious, like wanting more money, or great experiences, but many are hidden from our awareness, like wanting to feel loved, listened to, understood, or feel important, secure, or not be lonely.

Why is it important to be clear about our motives, both obvious and hidden, in any situation? These motives determine whether we regard any relationship or activity as successful or not. There may be motives we may not be aware of. You may join a meditation group, for example, and are not aware that deep down, you are lonely and looking to make friends. If you are not able to make any friends there, you will leave and may blame the group or the process of meditation for your dissatisfaction. The same applies to our relationships. If our hidden inner needs are not met, we may become unhappy and think that the other person is responsible.

On this journey of enquiry, therefore, it is important to be clear about what our motives are, both obvious and hidden, as we travel.

Eventually, the motives fall away, and the enquiry becomes part of you, like breathing. It is quite amazing when that happens.

OBSTACLES TO ENQUIRY

There are many obstacles that we may encounter on this journey of self-understanding. Exploring these beforehand may help us to avoid them. Some challenges may block our enquiry altogether while others take us down the wrong road, where there is no illumination.

Taking responsibility for how we feel is a challenge, and can be the first obstacle we trip over. It is important to accept and take ownership of our feelings of stress as they arise in us in reaction to an event or person. This allows us to study them. Our instinct, however, is to blame the situation or other person for how we are feeling. Our journey of enquiry can end before it even begins. Feelings just are, they are not right or wrong, or good or bad, or someone's fault, though there are exceptions I am sure. Understanding their origins in our thinking can bring illumination, insight, and change.

I may think I am a selfless person, for example, but as I observe myself, I realise that I am self-absorbed most of the time and think only about myself. I do not like what I see and cannot accept that this is who I really am, so I lose interest in the enquiry and stop looking. It may help to realise that we are the same as other human beings, and we are all self-absorbed to varying degrees. Letting go of our opinions of ourselves and accepting ourselves as we are is a crucial step if we are to learn more about ourselves.

Justifying who we are and what we feel is another common reaction. I regard all my thoughts and feelings as 'right' and will find reasons to justify them. That reaction blocks any further enquiry. It is built into the way our mind functions, but we need to move past that to continue exploring. "I am only human", we may say in response to noticing that we are feeling angry, but what we are really saying is that we do not want to enquire any further. Being critical of ourselves for being angry or justifying our anger as 'right' are both roadblocks to finding out what is behind my anger.

As we begin our enquiry, we may have certain expectations that this enquiry will help us in some way. Usually, these relate to our hidden emotional needs, which we will explore later in the book. We may feel that it will help us be less stressed or be happier or feel less lonely. If these expectations are not met, we may get disappointed and blame the enquiry process or this book, and move on to something else that meets our needs. It is important to be aware of our expectations and our needs, both obvious and hidden, as we engage with this enquiry. Can we engage with this enquiry without a specific goal in mind, perhaps just out of a sense of curiosity? As a consequence, we will never be disappointed because there is no destination that we are trying to reach.

What happens if we have engaged in this enquiry and found that we have not changed? How should we respond? Should we just give up or try and find out why we have not changed?

We could ask if we have enquired with passion, with an open mind, and been non-judgemental. Have we been honest with ourselves? Our hidden self-interest usually uses anything it can find to further its own needs. Have we been aware of that? If we have a mind that is continuously occupied or chasing something or in constant conflict, how can there be the space to discover anything new? This does not mean withdrawing from life or our relationships, but finding balance and space for the enquiry to flower.

There will be many occasions when you are inclined to give up and walk away from this enquiry. Remember, it is like learning to play the piano – challenging at first, but it becomes second nature as time goes on. It is a life-long journey of discovery and can enrich our lives in so many ways.

If something is different, it can feel strange, and that makes us reluctant to begin. Throughout our education, we were taught only about the world around us, but never to look at and understand ourselves, therefore, doing so now feels uncomfortable. No matter, what keep going.

We may worry about what we will find when we look at ourselves. This can make us anxious and reluctant to begin. Remember that deep down you are the same as all other human beings. All we have to do is take the first step, and then another one. Observe what is happening, ask why, and see what emerges. It is quite simple. We are just exploring the mind we human beings share, and there is no reason to feel afraid or anxious.

This enquiry may feel like it is only for 'clever' people or 'intellectuals' and we may not feel that we have the confidence to begin. We may not be literary people, and books may not be our thing. This enquiry does not need us to be clever or even educated, but just to have a passion for exploring our inner spaces and understanding ourselves as we are. Many riches await those who begin.

KEEP A JOURNAL

I have found that writing is an excellent way to understand what is going on in my thinking. I write about what I notice in the world around me, and what I observe in my thinking. A different part of my mind comes alive when I write, and it becomes quiet as I do so. My writing focuses on the discoveries I make as I look at myself. I have kept journals for many years and it has been a rich learning experience.

I sometimes ask a question, write it down, and then see what emerges in response. An example could be, "Why am I lonely? What is behind that feeling?" I keep my diary private so that I can be honest with myself. I go from the particular to the general, as I have described earlier in this chapter. I may begin by writing about a particular event, like feeling bad about what someone said, but then ask why, and explore the process behind that. I have discovered learning never ends because it is always fresh and in the moment.

INNER CAUSES OF STRESS

THERE ARE MANY PATTERNS OF thinking, often hidden from our awareness, which are common to all human beings and which play a role in the stress we experience. Self-understanding shines a light on them so that they do not operate in the background, and this awakens our inner intelligence, which in turn allows us to respond to challenges in the most appropriate way.

When a plane crashes, teams of investigators descend on the crash site to analyse what happened, retrieve and study the 'black boxes' to see what lessons can be learnt to stop similar crashes from occurring again. There is no culture of blame in the flying industry, so people are more open about problems and there is a spirit of learning and sharing of what may be discovered. It is logical and intelligent, and probably explains why flying is so safe.

We can apply a similar approach to when we feel stressed. We could study the cause of it and find out what we can learn. The cause of our stress may be in the world outside, say, for example, if someone is physically abusing us. Or, it could be coming from inside us, for example, from our need to feel important. If we really want to end our stress, we need to explore both of these possibilities (external and internal), and see what we can learn. The solution will then become clear and is easy to act on.

This approach requires us to change our attitude about stress, from a problem to be solved to an opportunity for learning about ourselves and the machinery of our thinking. In that exploration, we will discover that this machinery is the same in all human beings. It is also behind the creation of the sense of 'I' or 'me', as we will explore later. These discoveries have the potential to bring fundamental change.

CONDITIONING

Of all the inner causes of our stress, our conditioning is at the heart of most of them, so it is vital to understand how it operates in the background and how it can cause stress.

We store all our experiences from childhood onwards in our memory. We call this our conditioning. We are conditioned by our parents, the media, social media, newspapers, television, the society we grow up in, the religion of our parents, and so on. Some scientists argue that we are also conditioned genetically by the lives our parents led, and the science of epigenetics is exploring this phenomenon. Conditioning is not wrong but just needs to be understood.

We are not aware that we are conditioned. Our opinions are shaped by our conditioning, but we think they are original and are 'our' opinions. We do not realise that they are a synthesis of all our influences. For example, if you read a right-wing newspaper, you would have a particular view of immigration: that immigration should be reduced, that immigrants should be given fewer rights, or that they are responsible for taking jobs from the locals. If your partner reads a left-wing newspaper, their opinion would be different. They may think that they contribute to society, boost the economy, and provide cultural diversity which enriches the country. When you both meet to discuss the subject, you will not reference the newspapers you have read, but say that this is your opinion, and then try and convince each other that you are correct.

The advertising industry spends $550 billion per annum trying to influence our opinions, what we should buy, whom we should vote for, and they make use of the subtle nature of conditioning to do that.

If I am born on this side of the street in Belfast, in Northern Ireland, I grow up as a Catholic. You are born on the other side of the same street, and grow up to be a Protestant. We imbibe all the history of the conflict between our respective communities as children. We may grow up hating each other and never ask, "Why?" Conditioning can make us hate people we have never met. This animosity often lasts for lifetimes.

If someone I love leaves me for another, I get deeply hurt, and that conditions my future behaviour. I do not want to be hurt again, so I retreat into my shell, having only superficial relationships and not able to trust anyone.

Our views are shaped by the culture we grow up in. Now, we cannot imagine a time when women were not allowed to vote, but a hundred years ago, that was what men believed was correct for society. We cannot imagine now that they held those views. Or, if we go back 300 years when slavery was the norm, we cannot imagine how people thought that it was okay, but which they did and were fiercely resistant when their views were challenged. We are subtly conditioned by the society we grow up in without being aware that this is happening to us, and it shapes our view of the world. If we come across someone conditioned by different circumstances, there is potential for conflict, with each person certain that their view is correct.

Our conditioning subconsciously influences all our opinions, beliefs, aspirations, and behaviour as well. It also influences the clothes we wear, the food we eat and, what we regard as right or wrong. We regard all this is as normal. Anything that we encounter different from that norm can create a disturbance in our thinking, which we experience as stress.

Let me illustrate this with a personal example. When I first arrived in the UK from India, I came with two bits of conditioning. The first that I should look after my parents as they grew older and the second that women should do all the housework. You can imagine the conflict that caused. If I was challenged about these views, I would become defensive and give you many reasons why my view was justified. The more I was challenged, the more attached I became to my point of view. It was only when I began to question my conditioning that I realised that it was a good thing to look after my parents, and so I kept on doing that. I could, however, not justify the view that women should do all the housework, and so without any effort that just fell away.

The intelligent mind is aware that it is conditioned and notices how that influences every aspect of life. It is able to question itself without being attached to its own conditioning. It realises that conditioning is not wrong but just needs to be examined. In that awareness is the possibility of living with intelligence, and this brings change without effort, as in the example above.

OUR MIND IS REACTIVE

The human mind is reactive. Not always, just some of the time depending on the trigger. Having received input from all our senses, it compares what it has received with what it knows, and faster than a bullet coming out of a gun, it reacts. This reaction depends on the context. It is an essential function of the mind, designed to save us from danger. If we are crossing a road, and see a car coming at us from the corner of our eye, we can jump out of the way quickly. We react in the same way if there is a difference between our unconscious conditioning and what we see or hear.

This same process of thinking can also act to cause stress, for example. Our conditioning and our reactive mind combine to cause stress. You could say that stress is just the difference between the way things are and how we want things to be. The way we want things to be comes from our unconscious conditioning, to which we have become attached. We justify all our opinions and behaviours and think that they are correct.

You have a different opinion to mine on a subject I feel strongly about and try to convince me that you are right. You may think, for example, that global warming is not caused by the increase in greenhouse gases. We get into an argument, and we both get stressed.

I may feel there is too much to do at work and get stressed, but do not question why a colleague copes with the same workload without a problem.

My son is behaving in a way that I would not, partying too much for example, and I am critical and get stressed. I grew up without partying, think it is a waste of time and money, assume that my way of looking at things is correct, and we end up arguing.

What determines the strength of my reaction? Each person reacts differently to the same situation, like a delayed flight, for example. Why is that? Personal circumstances play a role. One person may be late for a wedding, and the other is just returning home. The overall state of agitation or disturbance in my mind also influences my reaction. If I am already mentally upset because I have had a difficult childhood with no love and regular abuse, or I have financial problems, or I had an argument with my wife that morning, my reaction to simple events is likely to be much more severe. In neighbourhoods where gangs operate and where young men have grown up in really challenging circumstances, the slightest provocation triggers a violent response. A teacher in England was stabbed by a student when he went to confiscate the student's mobile phone. This also explains road rage, where the simplest accident can elicit a violent response. If people have unhappy relationships at home, they carry that stress to work, and the slightest trigger elicits an exaggerated reaction.

How can we respond to this fact of the reactive nature of our mind, with intelligence?

COMPARISON

Our mind is conditioned and reactive and we, largely, go about our lives quite unaware of these processes working in the background. It also continually compares what it sees/hears with what it knows, and is not aware that it is doing so.

The process of comparison is essential for life. It allows us to identify dangers, such as a poisonous snake. It also allows us to recognise the people we have met before. Without comparison, we could not find our way home or do our jobs.

The same process of comparison, which is essential for living, can also be a cause of stress, and understanding this allows us to respond with intelligence.

Comparing ourselves with others generates pleasure; if I have a bigger house than you or more money, or am more important. This is behind ambition and the drive for success. The same process can also cause the pain of envy or jealousy. If someone has done better than me in the exams, or bought something I would have liked, I feel envious. This can happen even though you may be my best friend, and even if I do not want to feel envious. This is because the process of comparison and the envy it generates is unconscious and automatic.

It is one of the main reasons why social media causes stress. We now have many more people to compare ourselves with, in ways which were not possible in the past. We know in detail what people wear, the food they eat, how they look, what they own, and the trips they go on.

We can feel under pressure to conform, or feel inadequate, or end up disliking who we are, or hating others for posting about their lives online.

This process of comparison can also make us want to be like others, without realising it. I may suddenly start feeling like I want to go from a size ten to a size six, not realising it is because I am comparing how I look with pictures I saw in a fashion magazine. Or I start taking protein shakes because I want a muscular body and convince myself that this is what 'I' want to do. Or I start feeling dissatisfied with different parts of my body, and that anxiety makes me think that plastic surgery is the answer. I get unconsciously conditioned into thinking that way and feel a compulsion to get the surgery done, justifying it to myself and others. As a result of this compulsion, I overlook the risks involved. I do not realise that the underlying insecurity and conditioning, which make me get the surgery done, are not going to go away afterwards.

This process of comparison can make me think that my happiness lies in being better than others because that brings a burst of pleasure. I have been conditioned since childhood in this way because every time I did well in an exam or a race, I was praised. I carry this unconscious conditioning with me in life, trying to be better than others around me. I call this being ambitious and society applauds that. But I find that there is always someone who is better or has more than me. This creates stress. Even if I get to the top of the pile and am the best, the pleasure I feel is short-lived – for example, if I am the best tennis player. Being the best has its problems too. I may start feeling anxious about maintaining my position, and that causes stress.

Of course, this particular narrative does not apply to everyone, but some version of it does, and it illustrates how the unconscious and automatic process of comparison can impact our lives and cause stress.

How can we respond with intelligence to the presence of comparison in our thinking processes?

PREJUDICE

'An opinion not based on reason or actual experience' is the conventional definition of prejudice. Our prejudices can make us stressed if, for example, I have a prejudice against black people, and a black person becomes the prime minister of my country. Understanding where our prejudices originate from can bring freedom.

We never think that we are prejudiced, and only notice it in others. For ourselves, it is merely a very justifiable opinion.

We all have many prejudices we carry with us and are not aware that we have them or how we acquired them, but feel compelled to justify them to ourselves and others, and they can be a significant cause of stress.

Our prejudices originate from our unconscious conditioning. They are reinforced by the people we surround ourselves with, as well as by repeating them to ourselves and others. We do not question these prejudices, but regard them as firmly held facts.

We know that the mind is reactive and compares what it sees with what it knows.

If I live in a white neighbourhood, and some immigrants move in, who have a different skin colour, speak a different language, and have different customs, my mind compares what it sees with what it regards as normal, and I experience a disturbance in my thinking without realising why. In that context, my stress reaction is called racism. I say things like, "If only they would learn to speak the local language" or "They should dress like the rest of the people in this country" or "They should integrate and adopt the customs of the local people who live here". If others change to become more like me, then I would not be stressed. I do not see the process at work behind the scenes, which makes me think this way.

The same process is responsible for our religious prejudices. Anti-Semitism is centuries old and rooted in historical narratives which have been passed down from one generation to the next, without being questioned. Similarly, the conflict between Shias and Sunnis is also based on historical narratives, which have conditioned generation after generation of people. If we were all educated to question our unconscious conditioning influences, many of these conflicts could end.

It is up to each of us to explore our own prejudices, question where they came from, and ask if that is still an intelligent view to hold. If I challenge your prejudices, you will just become defensive, not speak to me anymore, or will justify them. It is when you question yourself that there is an option to live with intelligence, with freedom from all prejudices.

Most of us are concerned about what others think of us and know that we cannot be seen to be racist, homophobic, or anti-Semitic. So, we suppress those views, and pretend even to ourselves that we do not have them. We only reveal them when we are with people who think like us, and we feel safe that no one else will find out. They continue to bubble away beneath the surface and find a way of influencing our opinion and behaviour. They also express themselves when we are not in full control of ourselves, after a few drinks, for example. Because they are hidden, sometimes even from ourselves, they are never challenged and continue to exist, sometimes for centuries.

If we can understand the unconscious process of thinking that creates our prejudices in the first place, there is a real opportunity to be free of all of them, at once. Now, would that not be beautiful? It would reduce stress in our lives, and make the world a better place. A much better place.

THE NATURE OF PLEASURE

The human mind is wired to pursue stimulation and pleasure. The need for pleasure operates in the background and influences our thoughts and actions. We equate pleasure with being happy, so we naturally assume that the more pleasure we have, the happier we will be. We pursue it with all our energy.

When I ask people whom I speak to, about the one thing that they want from their lives, almost all of them say that they want to be happy. When I ask them about what makes them happy, most of the answers are linked to pleasure in some way: shopping, eating out, physical intimacy, falling in love, being wealthy, being successful, drinking, being with family or friends, and so on.

We also get pleasure when our ego or sense of 'self' is boosted, and this can happen in several ways: when we are praised, when we are better than others, feel important, get recognised by others, achieve something, or someone says, "I love you". I get pleasure when I can talk about myself, about my experiences and opinions. I also get pleasure from being critical of others because that is always relative to 'me' and is a subtle way of saying that I am better or different. I feel pleasure when I meet people who share my opinions and beliefs and who are like me. Once these patterns of pleasure get established, they tend to repeat themselves in our lives.

There is nothing right or wrong about pleasure, just a fact that needs to be explored and understood.

Unknown to us, the pursuit of pleasure can also cause stress and emotional pain. To understand why, we need to understand the nature of pleasure.

The possibility of pleasure in the future makes us feel happy in the present. The thought of buying something, earning more money, or meeting a romantic partner all bring pleasure. That gives us the energy to pursue that pleasure until we get whatever it is that we seek. Once we get what we want, the pleasure begins to fade, and we feel empty, dissatisfied, and restless again. The mind cannot cope with this, so it thinks of a new pleasure to pursue, and the cycle begins again. This time though, the same source of pleasure will not do. It has to be something bigger and better: a more expensive shoe, or a better phone, and so on. If I am into shoes, then that pattern repeats itself, and I end up buying more shoes. I met a lady recently who said she had 176 pairs of shoes. The fact that she knew precisely how many she had was surprising as well. Very soon, I have more shoes than I know what to do with, but feel unable to stop buying them. It could be shoes or clothes or alcohol or money or the pursuit of fame – the process is the same. When I am pursuing a certain kind of pleasure, all my critical thinking is side-lined, and even if a thought arises that says that I have enough shoes or books and do not need any more, I end up buying them anyway.

The need for pleasure is powerful and overcomes any obstacles we may put in the way. People who take a vow of celibacy struggle with this. There is a conflict between their ideal of celibacy, and the unconscious and ill-understood need for pleasure which can be an overwhelming force in our lives.

The mind that pursues pleasure eventually becomes dull, losing its sensitivity to itself, others, and the beauty of the world. If you watch video games all day, or spend all your time shopping, eventually the pleasure of it fades, and the mind becomes insensitive and dull. It loses its freshness and its ability to see and think clearly.

So, how can the pursuit of pleasure cause stress?

The pursuit of pleasure bypasses our critical thinking and makes us do things that are not intelligent: drinking too much alcohol, smoking, taking drugs, gambling, having unsuitable relationships, and so on. All these bring their own problems, which can result in stress.

If we cannot get something we desire, we can get stressed: being able to afford something we want, or a job, or the exam result we wanted, or a promotion at work. Any desire that is unfulfilled can cause stress. Behind all our desires is the hidden need for pleasure.

If we are looking for others to give us a pleasure boost by making us feel important, we can get stressed if that does not happen.

We are used to thinking about the past and reliving happy times we may have had, and that can bring pleasure. But for every happy memory that brings pleasure, there are also unhappy ones that bring emotional pain as we think about them, and that can cause stress. It is the same process that brings both pleasure and pain.

We become attached to people, pets, or things that bring us pleasure, and we can get anxious about the thought that they may one day not be there, or experience sorrow and emotional pain if we actually lose them.

How can we respond to this fact of the nature of pleasure, with intelligence?

To explore pleasure in this way requires us to stop thinking about it as good or bad or justify it as part of being human. That openness allows us to go deeper and see the many hidden ways in which it affects our lives. Learning about pleasure needs to happen in real-time, as it arises in us. This understanding awakens intelligence and it is this intelligence that responds appropriately to each situation such that pleasure has its rightful role in our life, and yet allows us to avoid the emotional pain and stress that often follows in its wake.

Our emotional needs

Our many hidden emotional needs can be a significant cause of stress. These operate from behind the screen of our awareness and influence our lives in many subtle ways. They are not right or wrong, just a fact that needs to be explored and understood so that we can respond with intelligence.

Some of our needs are to:

- Be loved
- Be listened to
- Be understood
- Express ourselves
- Be agreed with
- Not be lonely
- Feel important
- Experience pleasure
- Experience power
- Feel secure
- Be occupied
- Have new experiences
- Have a sense of peace

This is not a complete list, and you could add to it. Are we aware that we have these needs? How do they impact our lives? It is interesting to note that we have a need to be listened to, but not to listen to others, to be loved rather than be loving towards others, and so on. Why is that?

We expect these needs to be met by the world around us, through our jobs, relationships, hobbies, possessions, and so on.

What happens when these needs are met? We say, "I love you", "You are my best friend" or "I love this job" and so on. We become attached to anything or anyone that meets these needs – people, pets, jobs, titles, positions of power, objects like cars and our homes, as well as our opinions and beliefs.

What happens when these needs are not met? If I am in a relationship, without realising why I start to feel stressed, hurt, and unhappy, and think that it is your fault that I feel this way. I do not see that it is my own unmet needs that are causing my unhappiness. I react to that feeling and think, "Well, I am not going to meet her needs if she will not meet mine" or "I need to move on and find someone else" or

"This relationship is not working for me". If I am in a job, I start feeling stressed and blame the job for how I am feeling. I become disgruntled, start being critical of my job or my boss, and think that I need to move on and find another one. When I was working as a surgeon, I would often meet unhappy colleagues who said, "No one recognises all the hard work I do. It is a thankless job". There is nothing right or wrong about this, but illustrates how our hidden emotional requirements can make us feel unhappy and stressed if they are not met.

If I am expecting you to meet my emotional needs, and you are expecting me to meet yours, and neither of us is aware of this process, it is no surprise that there is a conflict between us. We will explore this in more detail later.

Because we are not aware of these needs, we never question them. For example, why do we want to feel important? Being important brings pleasure and boosts our ego, but it also hands the keys to our happiness to others, asking them to make us happy by making us feel important. If we do not feel important, we can become unhappy and stressed, often without realising why.

The subtle need for power brings pleasure and makes us feel more secure. It operates in the background. It could be as simple as 'winning' an argument, wanting to see the movie I want, or seeking political power. At work, there is always a subtle power game going on between 'winners' and 'losers'. What sort of an environment does that create? How well can people function if there is this constant power-play going on? It can result in fear, anxiety, resentment, and banishes goodwill. It does the same in our personal lives if it is not recognised. Because it operates unconsciously, we are not aware of its significance or the problems it can cause. As each person in a relationship jostles for power, conflict follows. If we can observe this happening in real-time and understand its significance, it awakens our inner intelligence that can respond appropriately. If we are not aware, we can use that authority for our own benefit, rather than serve the needs of the role we have, and that can lead to corruption. Some roles in life come with a certain authority: being a parent, or heading an organisation, or heading a government. If we can be aware of this unconscious need for power and pleasure operating in the background, we can respond with intelligence.

Consider an example of a couple I know; let us call them Jack and Diana. Jack insists on getting his own way and they have had several arguments over different issues through the years. Most recently, they were on holiday with friends. Every morning they would meet over breakfast to decide what to do for the day. Jack would insist that the group did what he wanted and it got very tiring for the rest of the group, and embarrassing for Diana. She got irritated with Jack and he got upset with her for pointing this out. The next day he tried to be a bit more accommodating but very soon 'took over' and was directing what the group did that day. He just could not help himself and was not aware of his behaviour or the reason behind it. He exercised subtle control over Diana in other ways: telling her what to wear, what to cook for dinner, whom she could meet and when, and so on. Their rows continued and their relationship became an unhappy one. Diana grew increasingly frustrated and resentful, and Jack got tired of their rows and could not understand the reason behind them.

These hidden emotional needs may also be behind our self-interest. When we meet other people, our unconscious thought is, "What can this person or organisation do for me?" or "How can I use this situation to meet my needs?" This is not right or wrong, but just needs to be understood, so it does not act in the background, corrupt our intentions, and make us do things we later regret like: using others to fulfil our need for pleasure, exercising power, harming others just to 'get ahead', or being dishonest in the pursuit of our own gains. In the short-term we may 'get ahead', but exploiting others for our own benefit is not a foundation for long-term happiness or living with peace.

Could these needs that we have also explain why we do not live with a sense of peace?

We are always looking for the next thing to occupy and stimulate us, and many of us are eternally discontented. Why is that? Our mind seeks new experiences all the time. Some regard it as the purpose of life, to gather new experiences and store them in our mind, so we can relive the pleasure they once brought. A mind chasing new experiences is a mind that knows no inner peace. It carries its deep discontent from one experience to the next, hoping that each new one will provide the answer it seeks. After each experience ends, the discontent returns, and we need a new one to take its place. This pattern becomes embedded in our thinking. We never question it because we do not see it.

Money has become so important in our lives because it can buy us new experiences, and the more money we have, the more exotic the experiences we can enjoy. It follows that if we do not have enough money to buy the experiences we want, we can get frustrated and stressed. If we have no shortage of money, after a while, these new experiences do not stimulate us enough to provide an effective escape from that gnawing ache inside us.

Seeking new experiences is not wrong, but we never ask what makes us seek them. Where do these needs come from and how do they impact our lives? Are they our responsibility or someone else's? Does the need to be listened to have the same root in our thinking as the need for power or the need to feel important, for example?

Perhaps all of these needs have a common source and they emerge from our deep sense of inner boredom that we do not often recognise within ourselves or admit even if we do. The pleasure that comes from getting our needs met covers this inner boredom, at least for a while. This process goes on far removed from our awareness and is common to all human beings.

An intellectual understanding of this process is a start, but brings no illumination or change. For that, each of us needs to observe, simply and without judgement, the way in which these needs operate in the background, the many ways in which they influence our lives, and the feeling of emptiness that lies behind them. They are not right or wrong, good or bad, just a fact that needs to be understood. By connecting with that deep sense of emptiness within us, making friends with it, and not escaping it, perhaps we can discover that sense of peace that so eludes us.

THE NEED TO BE OCCUPIED AND NOT BE LONELY

Our minds have a need to be occupied, and we find it challenging to sit quietly, doing nothing. Even if we can sit quietly somewhere, our thoughts keep buzzing away, like billiard balls, each triggering another one. Why is that? What implications does that have for our lives and can this process result in stress?

We need to always be doing something: talking to someone, browsing the internet, watching TV, working, or seeking new ways of being stimulated. This need may be behind the explosion in mobile phones with easy internet access, and explain why we spend several hours on them every day. They provide a constant stream of new stimuli, which we do not get from our real lives.

Where does this need to be occupied come from?

This is a question each of us must ask ourselves, stay with it, and see what emerges. When I ask the question, there is no answer, but it does result in a feeling of quietness within me. Perhaps at the core of our consciousness is this feeling of uneasiness at being still, which we are uncomfortable with. We move away from it by being occupied or by seeking pleasure or power.

We are usually not aware of this process going on within us, and if we cannot distract ourselves, we say things like "I am bored" or "I am depressed at having nothing to do" or we can get stressed.

The same core process can result in a feeling of loneliness. Being with people, talking to them, being able to express ourselves, and feel connected and understood, is our mind's way of covering our deep sense of emptiness, and that makes us feel good. There is nothing wrong with that. A mind that makes its peace with this inner emptiness experiences solitude. A mind that wants to connect with others and cannot, feels frustrated that its desire is not met and feels lonely. There is nothing 'right' or 'wrong' about this feeling of emptiness we all have, and we still need to act in the world and relate to people. This understanding can, however, help us do that with intelligence, with a sense of peace, and avoid the stress associated with it.

If we can observe that feeling of emptiness within ourselves, let it express itself fully, accept it and not move away from it, it transforms into a sense of peace. All the stress associated with being alone or unoccupied can just dissolve. Please test it for yourself and find out if this is true for you.

You do not have to sit in the lotus position and meditate with your eyes closed to explore this feeling in yourself. When you are just sitting quietly and find yourself reaching for the phone, this feeling of inner boredom or emptiness is quietly there in the background. Just notice it, allow it to come to the surface, let it be, and keep observing it. Do not give in to that feeling and reach for the phone, but do not suppress it either or move away from it because it feels uncomfortable. The feeling is also there when you reach for the TV remote, or think that you need to go on a holiday or buy a new phone. It is very subtle sometimes and needs all our attention to notice it. We are just learning about ourselves, being curious, and finding out what we can discover. Sometimes it is there in all its fury, like a storm, when someone we love leaves us and we feel overwhelmed by the sadness of it. Again, sit with that feeling, without resistance, allowing it to wash over you like a wave. Something quite amazing happens when you are able to do this. It transforms into a sense of quietness that feels peaceful.

Fear

From our earliest times on earth, fear kept us safe from the threats around us and became embedded in our thinking. In modern times though, that same process contributes to the considerable stress we feel. Understanding the mechanism of fear in our thinking allows us to respond with intelligence so that we can still protect ourselves when needed, and yet avoid fears which have no basis in reality.

We cannot 'make' our fears go away because they emerge from the same mind as the thought which says, "I want to get rid of fear". The person who constantly worries or suffers from anxiety cannot abolish it using willpower alone. Telling an anxious person, "Do not be anxious", does not work and can make them feel even more stressed. Understanding the root of fear can, however, awaken intelligence and bring change without effort.

To understand the mechanism behind our fear, consider the analogy of watching a scary movie in a theatre. We see all the images being projected on the screen, believe them to be true, and we can get frightened. We do not see the projector, and because we are in a closed space, the fear is all too real. Similarly, our mind can also project scary images in front of us such as the simple act of thinking about bad things that can happen in the future. We may believe in the possibility of these things coming true and can become frightened. We do not see that they are a projection of our own thinking.

Consider another analogy. When we have a scary dream at night, it seems very real and we can wake up frightened. It is entirely a creation of our thinking, but when we are in it, we cannot see that. When we wake up and realise that we have been dreaming, that the fears are not real, and that we can relax, then our fear ebbs away.

Both the examples above indicate that fear is a product of our thinking process, but once the fear takes hold, that is difficult to see.

I was exploring the subject of fear with some primary school children, and one girl said, "Fear is caused by our imagination playing up". Children have an amazing intelligence and insight that is just waiting to be awakened.

Because all the things that we are afraid of have not yet happened, they have no solution, so our worries never go away. If the process of fear is active in us, there is no shortage of things to be afraid of and we are limited only by our imagination. If I am worried about what my son is going to be like when he grows up, and whether he will get a good job, that worry never goes away. It can, however, stress me out in the meantime and make me put pressure on him to study harder, which could strain our relationship and put him under undue pressure.

If bad things have happened to us or those around us in the past, we can be afraid of them happening again. Fear conditions our behaviour and our thinking, and we are not aware that it has done so. We suffer because the memory of the painful event is kept fresh by our thinking, but also because of the fear that it could happen again. An example of this could be if we have been attacked in the past, or lost a loved one to cancer, or lost a job, or someone we love has left us.

Fear is usually linked to a loss of things I value today – my health, my loved ones, my job, my status, my images of myself, my wealth, my looks, and so on. I can only be afraid of losing a million dollars if I have it, not if I do not.

Some fears are obvious, but many of them operate in the background, behind the screen of our awareness, causing stress and dictating our thoughts and actions. It is worth asking, "What are my unconscious fears and how do they influence my life?"

To explore the subject of fear we have to let go of any assertions that it is right or wrong, or essential or justified. Our opinion does not matter.

What matters is to understand the mechanism behind it and observe how it operates in our lives. This awakens intelligence and allows us to do the right thing. For example, I do not need a fear of losing my job or falling ill in order to get some insurance, or a fear of being hit by a car in order to cross the road safely, or a fear of getting cancer in order to stop smoking. Common sense can do that equally well.

Fear can negatively affect our lives in a number of ways that we are not aware of. It can cause stress, damage our health (if long-term), can make us afraid of change, stifle the flowering of goodness, and change our behaviour towards others. Sometimes it can make us behave aggressively and this is behind much of the violence in the world. Human beings are so afraid of each other that we spend hundreds of billions of dollars on arms every year, while hundreds of millions of people go hungry. What makes us human beings so violent and so afraid of each other? I gave a talk once to an audience of several hundred people. I asked if one half of the room was so afraid of the other half, would they stop eating and buy guns instead? It is a crazy idea, but that is what countries do, and we have never questioned it because we have not understood deeply the nature of fear or our need for power. Of course, each country does it because the other one does, and that is because the human mind is the same in everyone in either of the countries. But it all begins in our thinking, and we are not aware of that.

Because we do not understand that fear deeply, we unconsciously use it to control the behaviour of others, beginning with children at home and at school. Do we ever pause to reflect on the implications of doing so? Does it condition our children to be fearful as they grow older? If I have been brought up with fear, it is likely that I will pass it on to my children and use it to control their lives and the choices they want to make for their future. Is it behind the anxiety and panic attacks that are becoming all too common? What is the atmosphere in an institution which uses fear as a way of controlling behaviour? Is there any sense of shared purpose, goodness, and goodwill there? Could it be one of the factors behind the epidemic of violence we see among young people in our cities? If they have been brought up with fear, it shapes their thinking and behaviour, and is one of the reasons they can be so aggressive and prone to violence.

How can we meet fear with intelligence?

We can start by observing the many ways in which it operates in our lives, and we can do so without judgement. We need to understand that it is based on our idea of what may happen in the future about the loss of what we already have, and that many of our fears are not real. We think our worry is caused by the thing we are worrying about, not realising that it is the hidden process in our thinking that is responsible.

Here are some questions we can ask, which may help us to respond with intelligence:

- How likely is it to happen?
- How many of my fears actually came to pass?
- Can I accept whatever happens? What will I do if it does happen?
- Can I do anything to take precautions against it happening?

What are the chances that my fears will come to pass? It helps me divide my fears into three groups:

- If the likelihood is rare, that I have cancer in my spine or a meteor is going to destroy the earth, for example, I can ignore it because it is probably my imagination playing up.
- If the event is inevitable, that I am going to die one day, for example, is there any point in being afraid of it? I just have to accept it otherwise I am going to spend a lifetime in fear. I also have to accept that if I am going for an exam, a driving test, or a job interview, there is a chance I may fail, and if I do, I will pick myself up and do it again. Acceptance is not easy, but it dissolves fear. If we can accept that life is uncertain, and we will face the challenges that arise in the future with confidence, then many of our fears can disappear.
- If I can do something to prevent it, for example, having a heart attack, then I will do so: eat in moderation, do regular exercise, and avoid smoking. It also helps to remind myself that most of my fears have never come to pass.

This does not mean that life does not present us with challenges that we will need to face. It does that all the time. Being afraid does not help us deal with them any better. This also does not mean that fear is 'bad' or 'justified'. By understanding the process of thinking behind it, we can respond with intelligence rather than automatically with fear.

Consider an example. One of the common worries we have is what others think of us, and we want to be accepted by our peers. I asked some students why that was so important to them:

"Otherwise, we would be alone", they said.

"What would happen if we were alone?", I asked.

"We would feel bad", they said.

"Is that why you are afraid of being alone?", I asked. They nodded in assent.

"How many of you have ever tried being alone?", I asked. There was silence.

No one had tried that. They were afraid of something they had not experienced.

"Try it and see", I said, "It may not be as bad as you think".

"How can we end the worry of what others think of us?", I asked.

"Accept that being alone is okay", they said. Acceptance dissolves fear.

Fear causes stress in a number of ways, and shapes our thoughts and actions without our being aware of it. A deeper understanding of its roots in our thinking can bring freedom and allow us to avoid much of the stress that fear can cause.

OUR IDEALS

Our inability to live up to the ideal of the person *we want to be* can be stressful. We can also get stressed if the world does not conform to our ideal of how we want it to be; if say, for example, we do not want there to be any income inequality in society. The process by which our ideals form and potentially cause stress is not a conscious one.

Some examples of your ideals in action could be wanting to be unselfish, or to be the perfect parent for your children, or wanting everyone around you to be happy. If your reality cannot match your ideal, you could get stressed, without understanding why. You assume that your stress is caused by your inability to be the perfect parent, for example, so you try harder. No matter how hard you try though, you always seem to fall short. This causes stress and erodes your self-confidence.

Your ideals may extend to others, expecting people to have the same standards as you. For example, you may expect others to be as liberal and broad-minded as you are, and if they fall short, you could get stressed.

Where do these ideals come from? Did we arrive at them after careful consideration or did they just appear one day? They are not wrong, but they just need to be understood. Are they helpful in any way? Do they help us be a better version of ourselves? Why do we hang on to them? Perhaps there is another way to approach the subject, by understanding the hidden process behind them.

Our ideals emerge from our unconscious conditioning influences. They may be linked to our childhood, the society we are in, our religion, or the media. Because we are not aware of our conditioning, we never question our ideals and justify them to ourselves and others. They become part of our identity, the 'I', and get reinforced through repetition.

When we are unable to match the ideal of who we want to be, we get stressed, and can feel like a failure. We may get stressed because we do not think that we are the perfect parents. We do not realise that the actual stress is being caused by our ideal of what a perfect parent looks like, which we never notice or question. Our stress is just the difference between who we are and who we want to be. We assume it is who we are that is the problem, not realising it is who we want to be that is the cause of our stress. If we can let go of our ideal of who we want to be, and just accept ourselves as we are, all our stresses can dissolve.

The other advantage of letting go of our ideals is that we become grounded in reality. For example, we may have an ideal that we should not be racist or prejudiced. The ideal can cover the reality that deep down we are prejudiced, which we may not be aware of. These prejudices express themselves intermittently when we are not looking. Letting go of our ideals allows us to look at ourselves as we are, accept our prejudices and explore them. As our enquiry continues, we see that they are linked to our unconscious conditioning. This understanding awakens our intelligence, which brings change and freedom from all our prejudices.

Paradoxically, letting go of our ideals not only allows us to be free of the stress of living up to them, but can also bring transformation because we have explored their origins in our thinking. We can change not by creating an ideal and chasing it, but by accepting and exploring the fact, which in turn brings illumination. An analogy to explain this could be a dirty table, which we cover with the clean tablecloth of our ideals, and convince ourselves that it is clean. The table is still dirty, but the fact is hidden from view. By seeing clearly that the table is dirty and cleaning it, there is no need of an ideal to aspire to.

When I was young, I was enamoured with the ideal of non-violence. These ideals are as old as the hills, 'Turn the other cheek', for example. If I was able to match up to this ideal, I would be happy and wear it as a badge as part of my identity. When I did not meet my ideal, I would be critical of myself and say I needed to try harder. As I started to question myself, I realised that I was still violent, but this was being covered over by my ideal of non-violence. I had convinced myself that I was noble and good and non-violent, but that was an illusion. I let go of the ideal and asked myself, "What are the roots of violence in my thinking?" This violence did not mean that I hit people, but it manifested subtly, like hurting others with words. I understood that violence can be a response to hurt, fear, greed, my beliefs being challenged, a need for power, and so on. As I explored all these roots of violence in my thinking, the violence in me ebbed away. One day I realised that there was very little violence left in me, so there was no need to be non-violent, and that ideal also dissolved.

I met a lady who had a young child and worked full-time. Motherhood is a challenging time for everyone: juggling the various priorities of work, home, and looking after children. She was always stressed because she wanted to be the perfect mother, and wife, have the perfect home, and also be excellent at her job. Her stress came from not matching up to her ideal of who she wanted to be. She could not see that it was her ideals that were causing her stress. She felt inadequate as a mother, did not think that she was a good wife, and felt that she was not doing justice to her job. Even after she was made aware of the real cause of her stress, she felt unable to give up her ideals of who she wanted to be, just enjoy being a mother, and do things as best as she could.

I see that the more ideals I have of the person I want to be, the greater the chance that I will be stressed or disappointed. Our ideals get woven into our sense of identity and who we think we are. That is why we become attached to them and cannot let them go. Seeing this awakens intelligence and can bring transformation.

OUR IMAGES OF OURSELVES

These operate in a similar way to our ideals, in that the process is beyond our awareness, but with some differences. It is thus worth exploring separately. While our ideals reflect who we want to be, our images are the opinions we hold about ourselves. We are often not aware of them and they may not be accurate. These could include:

- I am successful
- I am important
- I am wealthy
- I am a good teacher or cook
- I am a good actor or musician
- I am well respected
- I am a good parent
- I am funny

We do not consciously decide to have these images. They just accumulate in us through our conditioning. How do they cause stress?

We strive to live up to our images of ourselves and want others to acknowledge them and reinforce them. When that happens, it brings a subtle pleasure, and we are happy. This striving starts to unconsciously influence our behaviour. For example, you may turn the conversation to golf, and talk about the wonderful round you played the other day. You want other people to engage in that conversation and acknowledge that you are a good golfer. When these images are not acknowledged by others, you can feel stressed and not understand why. When they are challenged and someone says you are a poor golfer, for example, the stress this causes can be acute. Examples here could include: if there is a bad press review after your musical performance, or if you fail at something, or you become less important than you were.

We gather around people who reinforce our images and avoid those who do not. These images influence our choice of friends and work colleagues whom we want to spend time with.

How can we respond with intelligence to these facts and the very process of image-making itself? The first step is to become aware that this process is operating in us and to notice the many different ways in which it influences our lives. It is not right or wrong, it just needs to be understood. We can also see that the more images we have of ourselves, the more chances there are of us getting hurt or stressed, even though they bring a subtle pleasure when reinforced. We may decide to let go of them or at least become aware of these images as they arise in us, and then meet them with awareness and intelligence.

OUR EXPECTATIONS

Our expectations of others and the world we live in are a significant cause of our stress, and understanding them can help us avoid so much of it. There are similarities with our images and ideals in the way they operate in the background and influence our life.

In all our relationships, we develop expectations of how others should behave and when they do not, we can get hurt or distressed. We are usually not conscious of these expectations and often only become aware of them when we feel hurt. These expectations have their origins in our unconscious emotional needs which we expect others to meet, as we discussed earlier.

Here are some examples of the unconscious expectations we have, and when they are not met, we can get distressed:

- I expect my friend to call or come and meet me
- I expect the person I am in a relationship with to understand what I am thinking or feeling
- I want my boss at work to make me feel important
- I expect my children to make a fuss over me on my birthday
- I expect others in the house to do their share of the housework

- I expect others to do what they said they would
- I expect to be emotionally supported, and loved, and understood

Where do these expectations come from? Are they our responsibility or do we expect others to meet them? Are we even aware that we have them?

And, how do we respond when these expectations are not met? We usually blame others, get hurt, get stressed, and think of retaliating in some way. The same expectations continue to operate and create the same reaction each time. Somehow, we cannot break that pattern, however much we want to. Why is that? Are we even aware that there is a pattern continually repeating itself?

If we observe how our minds function, we find that we are mostly concerned about ourselves. We spend most of our time thinking about our own needs and how to meet them. How much time do we spend thinking about the expectations that others have, and try to fulfil them? If you ask me to do something for you, I am usually more than happy to do so, but if you expect me to read your mind and anticipate your expectations and meet them, I feel lost. We are usually unable to articulate our expectations because we are not aware that we have them. Even if we are aware, expressing them feels like a sign of weakness, and since we are afraid of the other person's response, we often say nothing. If we are in a relationship, we expect the other person to understand our needs and meet them, even if we do not understand them ourselves; and we can get upset if the other person does not respond as we expect they should. That does not sound very rational, but it happens all the time.

Perhaps it is helpful to realise that we are the same as other human beings and they too spend their lives thinking mostly about themselves, just as we do. They do not have the time or space to be concerned about us, much as we would like them to. If we do not understand our unconscious expectations and cannot articulate them, why should we expect others to understand them? If this is clear, then it follows that if we have a long list of expectations of others, which are mostly unconscious, then we are going to get upset. So, what are we supposed to do?

How can we respond to the facts that we have uncovered with intelligence? A tempting response is to say, "We should not have expectations".

It does not work. Try it and see. Our expectations emerge from an unconscious space where our willpower cannot reach.

Instead, we could begin by becoming aware of the many expectations we do have. We could then examine them, take responsibility for them, and at least not blame others for not meeting them. Our expectations emerge from our own thinking, so they are our responsibility, however justified we may think them to be. It is not intuitive or easy to accept this, but an essential first step if we are to continue exploring them. Taking responsibility for our expectations has one other benefit – it stops us from reacting with anger when they are not met.

This does not mean that we cannot share how we are feeling with the people in our lives. You can tell a friend you felt hurt that they did not contact you when they were in town, but not get angry and resentful about it. If you can tell me what your expectations are and I can tell you mine, at least we can have an open conversation about them, and if we are in a loving relationship, try and meet them, not from a sense of obligation and pressure, but from a place of affection and care. It is difficult to have these conversations, but they are essential to keep our relationships healthy.

For any enquiry to proceed, we need to understand what is the fact and what are our opinions about the fact. The fact is that we have expectations that we expect others to meet, and when they are not met, we get hurt, angry, and stressed. Our opinion about the fact could be that expectations are normal and justified, or that they are wrong and only cause pain, or that we should not have any, or that people in relationships should meet each other's expectations. If we can put our opinions to one side and just explore the facts, it allows new insights to emerge. For example, we may find that behind most of our expectations is a need for pleasure or some form of self-fulfilment. We could observe our expectations, watch how they first come into being, and how they influence our lives. We can then see that the more expectations we have of people or how we want the world to be, the more likely we are to be disappointed and stressed.

One other process behind our expectations is that we want the world to be a mirror of who we are. We expect others to behave like we would, share our opinions and beliefs, and when this does not happen, we can get stressed. We have earlier explored the implications of this reactive process and how we can meet it with intelligence.

Through this enquiry into our expectations, an enquiry without judgement or an endpoint, we may find that something has shifted within us. Our expectations do not operate hidden from our awareness, as they once did, and we can meet them with intelligence, so they no longer have the power to cause us emotional distress. Even if they do, we recover quickly because we understand the underlying process.

I can vouch for the fact that this approach works.

OUR NEED TO BE LIKED

Many of us worry about what others think of us. We want to be liked and be part of a group. If others think negatively about us, it can cause stress because the urge to be part of a peer group is strong. We are worried that we might end up being alone. The fear of being excluded from a group can cause anxiety and make us alter our behaviour to 'fit in'. We may not be comfortable doing so, but do it anyway. Being part of a group fulfils many of our emotional needs. We feel less alone, think that others will protect us if there is a problem, feel important if we are in a position of authority, and can feel secure. All this process happens unconsciously, beyond our awareness. This need that we have to be liked by others is not right or wrong, but just a fact that needs to be understood. At present this need operates in the background influencing our behaviour, creating expectations, and when these are not met, results in stress. Becoming aware of this unconscious process allows us to respond consciously and with intelligence. We could question this need in ourselves, see how it is a potential cause for stress and can result in anxiety, and then decide what we want to do.

Why do we like some people and not others? People can have entirely different opinions of the same person. Why is that? We like people who share our interests, opinions, and beliefs, and who meet our unconscious needs. Just as we are quite selective in the people we like and do not like, others are too, and it is no wonder that we will be liked by some people and not by others. We also do not seem to have any conscious control over this process and cannot force ourselves to like someone against our instincts. This is the same in others. Why do we sometimes get upset when some people do not like us? Perhaps we need to accept that it is just not possible to be liked by everyone, and those who dislike us are not 'bad' people.

Our perception of ourselves is always different from that of others. You may not realise that you are a poor listener, for example, or that you subtly try to show off your achievements. This is why any feedback from others should always be welcomed.

Why do some of us need others to like us, to feel okay about ourselves? Is it because we feel insecure? Are we even aware of it, and where does that feeling come from? That feeling of insecurity could push us to buy the latest clothes to 'fit in' with the popular culture, even if we cannot afford them. Despite having plenty of friends and a wardrobe full of smart clothes and shoes, this feeling of insecurity never goes away. It just gets covered up and continues to operate from behind the scenes. Living with this insecurity creates a low-level anxiety about what others think of us, and in that there is no peace.

What can we do to understand why we feel insecure and are anxious about what others think of us?

The first step is to become aware of how this sense of insecurity operates in your life. Just notice it, without judging it or trying to change it. You may realise that this feeling follows you everywhere. You realise that this insecurity makes you uncomfortable and behind it is a fear of being alone and left out. It does not feel easy to turn around and face it. When it arises in you, sit quietly and just remain with the feeling, not escaping from it. You may realise that you have never explored being alone before and are afraid of something you have not tried. You could just sit down on your own sometimes and just watch the world go by. Initially, it feels difficult and you have a strong need to do something and be occupied. As you continue observing the feeling, accepting it and relaxing into it, the feeling itself transforms.

You may discover that sometimes you are now happy to be alone and enjoy your own company. You do not crave the constant attention or validation from others or to keep buying new clothes. You may not have the same urge to fit in, though you are still sociable and get on with everyone. You could accept that some people will like you and others will not. You may accept yourself as you are and become comfortable in your own skin. To your surprise, you may find that there is a sense of peace within. This process of being comfortable with being alone does not lead to isolation, but that feeling of insecurity and anxiety about what others think goes away. You may no longer feel compelled to belong to a group where you are not entirely comfortable.

This change does not always come about by your wanting to change. It could begin with an idle curiosity to find out what is going on inside of you. When you find that your insecurity was behind so much of your stress, you could begin to ask questions and explore it further. Understanding what is going on awakens an inner intelligence in you, and to your surprise, you may find that you have changed.

This ability to be comfortable being alone and accept who we are does not come naturally to us. We can discover it by exploring our sense of insecurity, our fear of being alone, and our need to belong to a group and conform. It can address a major cause of stress in our lives. You have to give your heart to this enquiry. It is simple, but not easy.

CRITICISM

We are all familiar with the searing pain we can feel when criticised. Have we ever paused to look under the hood and figure out why we feel this pain, what is the process of thinking behind it, and if there is an intelligent way to respond? What is going on in our thinking that makes us critical of others? And why are we so often critical of ourselves? This can cause low self-esteem.

Understanding the unconscious mechanisms behind criticism can bring illumination and allow us to respond with intelligence.

Why are we critical of others? We have explored previously how the human mind is conditioned and reacts to the world from that narrow slice of conditioning, comparing what it sees with what it knows. This is an unconscious process, and we assume that our opinions, beliefs, and ideas are correct because they originate in our thinking. Anything we find that is different most often creates a disturbance in our thinking and we can respond by being critical of the other person or situation. We express that criticism if we are not afraid of them: our children, partners, politicians, and subordinates at work. We are rarely openly critical to friends for fear of losing their friendship or to people in positions of authority. We are not aware of this process going on in the background. Our criticism reveals more about us than about the person we are critical about.

Here are three reasons why we may enjoy being critical of others. First, it reinforces our sense of 'self' and our ideas and beliefs. That brings a certain pleasure. We feel we are 'right' and others are 'wrong'. Second, being critical of others sometimes also involves having a subtle sense of power over them, and this can bring pleasure. Lastly, if I am critical of you and you change, then I can feel more comfortable because the disturbance in me goes away.

Consider an example of a man whom we shall call Adam. If Adam has grown up in a conservative country where homosexuality is banned, his views are shaped by that conditioning. If he comes across a gay couple being physically affectionate in public, it creates a disturbance in his thinking, and he has a critical reaction. It occurs automatically without thinking. He is certain he is right, and they are wrong. His criticism reinforces his opinions and beliefs about homosexuality, and his sense of personal identity. If he is openly hostile towards the gay couple, that sense of power brings pleasure. If, as a result of his criticism, they change, then the disturbance in his thinking goes away and he can be at peace. This is an obvious example, but people can be critical of each other over the smallest details as well, like how they dress, or their opinion about a certain politician, or how they use the toothpaste. The process is the same and happens automatically and unconsciously.

How criticism affects children is worth exploring because it is all too common and can have unintended consequences. It is, of course, sometimes essential to tell a child what is right and wrong and this is an important part of learning and growing up. What we do not realise is that our criticism is sometimes aimed at making them more like us. We can do this without thinking, on autopilot, and thus without any conscious regard for the consequences.

Too much criticism can damage a child's self-esteem and confidence and create a chasm between the parent and the child. We are unaware of the process behind it, sometimes giving a running commentary on how things should be. This may make the child afraid of the parent, or resentful because being criticised is hurtful. This may cause lasting psychological damage to the child, making them fearful and lowering their self-confidence. Sometimes all it generates is resentment, especially if one is dealing with teenagers.

With this understanding, how can we offer feedback and criticism with intelligence? There are times when we need to tell children and the people that we live or work with that we are not happy with the way things are and make suggestions for change. *How* we do it is the key, and we need to learn to do it well. The first step is to be aware of the hidden process behind it, operating in the background, and the potential it has to cause harm. When our criticism is automatic, unconscious, and reactive, it is usually laced with irritation or anger. The other person responds to the tone of our voice, as much as to what we are saying, and reacts negatively. When possible, criticism is probably best shared separate from the acute event, so that we are not irritated when we offer it.

Here are some questions to consider when offering criticism:

- Is it justified?
- Is the other person just different, rather than wrong?
- What would happen if I did not say anything?
- Does it really matter?
- Is it just a reaction from my particular conditioning?
- How is it going to be received?
- How is the person likely to react?
- Am I afraid of that reaction? Is it important to say it anyway?
- If I want the person to change, is this the best way of going about it?
- Can I balance the criticism with appreciating something about the person?
- Is it kind?

Criticism can cause hurt, resentment, and anger, so it is right that we consider it carefully before offering it.

How do we respond when we are criticised? Reactions vary widely, depending on the personality of the person and the context. Some people respond poorly to the slightest criticism, while others are more robust. Our reaction depends on how we are feeling at the time. If we are generally disturbed because of other reasons, we can respond with fury. We usually feel hurt, and that feeling can make us lash out and be angry, or become defensive and justify what we are doing, or be critical of something we do not like about the other person. We also store the memory of the hurt and allow it to affect our behaviour towards the other person in the future. Repeated criticism may make us hypersensitive and react disproportionately to the slightest negative comment. If we have grown up with criticism and been hurt by it, we can become anxious about any situation where we may receive some. Some teachers I have met say that they have been anxious and not slept for a week before a formal assessment because of their fear of being judged.

We are not critical of everything people say. If I am a florist and you are critical of my floral arrangements, I will get upset. But if you are critical of my singing, I may laugh and agree with you, and say that I need some singing lessons. What is the difference? Perhaps it is because I have an image of myself as a good florist, but no image of myself as a good singer. Being a good florist is part of my identity, the 'me', and when you are critical of anything I identify with, I feel hurt and react accordingly. I identify with my opinions, my religion, my country, my political party, my profession, and my family. If you are critical of any of them, it feels like you are attacking 'me'. The more images I have of myself and the more things I identify with, the greater the risk that criticism will make me feel angry and defensive. The pain of that feels every bit as real as if you were physically attacking me.

How can we respond to being criticised with intelligence?

The first step is to be aware of the ache we feel when we are criticised and understand the process of thinking behind it. We could put aside our initial reaction of hurt and ask ourselves if there is any truth in what is being said. If there is, we could be grateful to the person because it may help us improve. We are usually unaware of our behaviour and others can see things that we may have overlooked. We may be drinking too much, for example. It is often difficult for people to offer us any criticism because they are afraid of our reaction. The smart thing to do may be to invite negative feedback from the people closest to us. This has many benefits. Firstly, it keeps our closest relationships healthy, and if there are any problems, we can deal with them straight away. It also allows us to reflect on who we are, how we are being perceived, and make any changes that we think are appropriate. The ability to receive criticism with intelligence is also valued by all employers. This does not mean that we accept all criticism as valid, but at least we are no longer afraid of it and can then use our intelligence to decide what to do with it. It is especially important if we are in any position of authority because people are naturally afraid to tell us what they think. If they cannot speak up, we cannot be effective and may make serious mistakes in our decision making. Many leaders fail because of their inability to accept criticism and create an open environment where feedback is encouraged. This acceptance and openness may seem difficult at first, but after some time it becomes second nature.

Why are we sometimes critical of ourselves? People can suffer all their lives because they think that they are 'not good enough', or think that they are a 'failure', or cannot break a habit they want to. It can cause low self-esteem, a loss of confidence, and stress. What is going on and why do we feel that way? We may unconsciously compare ourselves unfavourably with friends, and think that we are not as popular as others, for example. Others may get invited to more parties and generally seem to be having a 'good time'. Or, we may feel that we get stressed too easily or we are not good parents, and this can make us feel inadequate and critical of ourselves. We think that the problem is who we are, but do not realise that the problem lies in who we want to be, which in effect has come about through various unconscious patterns of thinking, like comparison and conditioning. If we see that clearly, we can let go of who we want to be, accept ourselves as we are, and all the self-criticism melts away.

How can I improve as a person if I am not critical of myself? Does self-criticism not help me change for the better? Consider two examples.

A young man realises that he spends too much time on his phone. He watches TV programmes late into the night and wakes up at midday. Try as he will, he cannot break this habit, and he is critical of himself for not being able to do so. Any suggestions as to how he could help himself are met with resistance. The cycle continues. His self-criticism makes him feel depressed, and this compounds the problem.

A young woman is happy most of the time but can lose her temper at the slightest provocation. If she is doing something and it is not perfect, she gets angry with herself and expresses it in inappropriate ways, by banging doors, for example. When she calms down, she is self-critical for what happened. The cycle continues.

Real change comes from first accepting what is going on and then calmly exploring what lies behind that behaviour. Being self-critical without understanding the root of the problem in our thinking rarely results in transformation. In the examples above, it may mean exploring why the mind likes to be occupied and continually stimulated, for example, or exploring our ideals of perfection.

Self-critical people are usually critical of many aspects of their lives. Having an insight into this hidden process at work awakens intelligence, and this can bring transformation.

MISTAKEN PERCEPTION

Two people are walking down a path in a forest. One sees a snake and jumps back with alarm. The other person sees a rope and keeps walking.

A policeman hears a sharp sound and assumes that it is a gunshot and draws his gun, ready to shoot. A person walking by thinks it is a firecracker and keeps walking.

Both these examples illustrate how our perception defines our reality and determines how we feel and respond. Both people in the two examples above cannot be right. It is either a snake or a rope, and either a firecracker or a gunshot.

In daily life, our perceptions are sometimes mistaken, and we end up getting stressed without due cause. It is important, therefore, to understand the factors that can influence our perception of a situation. This can help us see things clearly as they are, and respond with intelligence.

Our perception is most obviously influenced by our conditioning. Most of us are not aware of this and assume that what we initially think is always right. In the examples above, the policeman is conditioned by his time spent dealing with crime and assumes that the sharp sound is a gunshot. The person who sees a snake may have seen a programme about them recently, for example. Or, if I am a child in a playground and I see others talking a distance away, laughing, and someone glances at me, I assume that they are talking about me and I get anxious and upset. The truth may be that they were talking of something completely different, but my automatic response does not consider that possibility.

Perception is also influenced by how positively or negatively we see the world. Many people see the glass half empty and are likely to think the worst in a situation. For example, if a friend did not call when they said they would, I could assume that it is because they do not care anymore, but the truth may be that their phone ran out of battery. It follows that those who have a negative mindset are more likely to suffer stress.

With this understanding, what is the intelligent way to respond? I could ask myself if I see a situation clearly and if there is another way to look at it. The very question awakens intelligence. My initial perception may be incorrect and based exclusively on my conditioning. We can avoid a lot of stress by questioning our initial response to situations.

CONFLICT IN OUR RELATIONSHIPS

There is so much avoidable suffering in all kinds of relationships caused by conflict. This is equally true of romantic relationships, and our relationships with siblings, parents, children, co-workers, and friends. This is sometimes caused by unconscious patterns of thinking which are common to all of us, and understanding them could help us avoid them. In the US, divorce rates are between 40–50% and are similar in many countries. For every divorce, there is another relationship that is not entirely happy. Why do we human beings struggle to have happy relationships? It is, after all, the one thing all of us want. Why have we been unable to use our incredible intellect to bring about happy relationships?

Conflicts occur in all relationships. In every dispute, each person blames the other, but unknown to us, the patterns of thinking that generate conflict are the same in everyone. Being aware of them can help us avoid the stress associated with them.

Differences of opinion can cause conflict. This includes everything from our political views, to where to hang a picture on a wall. Though opinions differ, the process by which our opinions form and the reason we get attached to them are the same. Our views emerge from our narrow slice of conditioning, which is the sum of all our experiences. We become attached to whatever emerges from our mind as 'ours', and do not want to give ground, even for something trivial. If there is a difference between what you and I want, there is resistance and potential for conflict. If we could realise that this unconscious process is the same in both of us, we could yield with grace. Seeing this process at work, I may ask myself if it really matters where a picture is hung on a wall, or what my opinion is, for example, and just let it go. A useful question that may illuminate our differences could be, "Why do we think this way? Where do our different opinions come from?" That may lead to a discovery of their roots in our unconscious conditioning influences, which may shift our perceptions.

When we look at people we are related to, we compare what we see with what we know, and any difference we find creates an unconscious disturbance. Without realising it, we respond to this in three common ways.

We can get irritated and are critical of what the other person is thinking or doing, and this creates a corresponding reaction where they become critical of what we are doing, or they get irritated or angry with us. If I say that I do not like your oranges, you could respond by saying that you do not like my apples, and the conflict continues without resolution.

We try and change the other person to conform to our view, and to be more like us. If they changed, the disturbance in our thinking would end. If I am a vegetarian and we are in a relationship, it disturbs me that you eat meat, and I try to change you so that I can feel more comfortable. You may try to convince me of the benefits of eating meat, resulting in conflict. We can try and change others in several ways:

- If I am the more powerful person in the relationship, earning more money, for example, I can simply insist that this is what we are going to do. That creates resentment, and the fragrance of affection between us disappears.
- Or I may give you many reasons why being a vegetarian is better and you try and convince me of the benefits of eating meat, and our conflict continues.

- Or I may agree to compromise and eat meat, but want you to agree to do something I want in return.
- Or I may be critical of you each time you eat meat, and this makes you angry, and our conflict escalates.
- Or I may withdraw my affection from you, in retaliation, because you are not willing to change.
- Or I may try emotional blackmail and say, "If you loved me you would give up eating meat".

Every time I sense that you are trying to change me, it creates resistance, and that sows the seeds of conflict between us. If we could wake up and become aware of this process at work behind the scenes, which is the same in both of us, we could respond with awareness, and much of our conflict could end. Can I let go of my *attachment* to my opinions that emerge from my unconscious conditioning? Without this attachment, I could willingly accept the differences between us with serenity. If I can yield with grace, the other person is also much more likely to do so.

Another major cause of conflict between people in a relationship is our unmet emotional needs. We are not aware that we have these needs and expect the other person to meet them. If you meet my emotional needs, I am happy and willing to do anything for you, but if they are not met, it creates stress and conflict between us. We have explored this in a previous section. If I expect you to meet my needs, and you expect me to meet yours, and we are not aware of this process at work in the background, conflict is inevitable. Even if I am aware of them, I feel unable to communicate these needs to you because that makes me feel vulnerable and anxious. So, I expect you to understand what my needs are, and meet them, without me having to share them with you. If you do not meet my needs, I decide not to meet yours, and the distance between us grows. The stage is set for escalating conflict, which may end the relationship. These needs are not wrong, but they need to be understood and discussed. In that discussion, we would realise that they are the same in both of us. The understanding of this hidden process at work allows us to respond in a fresh way, and our conflicts and the stress they generate could be significantly reduced. We may go on to examine these needs together, letting go of the ones that make no sense – our need to feel important or have power, for example.

When we feel that we are not being listened to or understood, we can get upset. Communication is the foundation of all successful relationships. Without effective communication, there is no connection, and relationships can quickly become a conflict zone, making people drift apart. Our education does not teach us the art of communicating well, so we are not good at it. This subject is covered in more depth in a previous book of mine, but I will explore the salient points here.

Up to 80% of our communication is non-verbal, beyond language. Communication is affected by the tone of our voice, our body language, and whether we are agitated in some way, or not. We are usually not aware of this. If I am irritated with you, you sense that and react accordingly, irrespective of what I may be saying.

We could be better listeners. Why do we have such a strong need to express ourselves but not the same need to listen? When we listen, our mind reacts to what we are hearing, and an automatic response emerges from our thinking. As this happens and we wait to express ourselves, we stop listening. This response has tremendous energy behind it. We are confident that we are right. We interrupt others to express ourselves. We also get easily distracted, do not make eye contact, are reactive, and do not try to understand the meaning behind the words being spoken. We scan a conversation to look for something of interest to us. If it is not interesting, we can switch off and start thinking of something else. It is not easy to continue listening deeply to someone who is saying something we disagree with. By realising that we do not listen well – and all the reasons behind that – we could become better listeners. The understanding does all the work of bringing transformation.

When we speak, do we ever pause to consider how it is going to be received? We rarely do this because the urge to speak is powerful and automatic. This simple question can prevent many conflicts in communication. If what we say or how we are saying it is not going to have the desired effect, we could keep quiet or find a different way to communicate. Do we need to say anything at all? In future conversations, try asking yourself this question. You might be surprised by what answers arise.

When a person is speaking, we need to understand what the other person *means* and how they are *feeling*, and not just rely on the words being used. We often react to the words being spoken, rather than try to understand the meaning behind them. The other person ascribes a meaning to their words based on their conditioning, but we interpret the words based on our conditioning. This is how misunderstandings occur. Also, the words do not always convey the entire truth of what the other person means to say. A person who is listening deeply understands this and asks questions to clarify.

We do not see people freshly but through the screen of our memories of them. This is an unconscious process. If we have been hurt by someone before, sometimes even years ago, that memory is alive and affects our behaviour towards the other person. We may withhold our warmth and affection. The other person senses that something is not right and responds equally coldly. Others view us through the screen of their images of us. In all relationships, as memories of hurt and disappointment accumulate, the emotional distance between people grows larger and drives out real affection, warmth, and goodness. This may explain why, over time, many relationships deteriorate into conflict, even if people stay together. Letting go of these accumulated memories of hurt is crucial if we want to have relationships without conflict. We are all continually changing, so it is important to see people freshly. The person who is aware of this process works at putting old images and memories aside, and meets the other person freshly, in the present.

Anger

If we are being assaulted, anger is essential to protect us from harm and is a core human emotion. Like water, which is essential for life but can also cause flooding, anger too is part of being human but can cause problems in our lives. It can damage our relationships, cause stress, and end in violence.

Having an insight into our anger and its origins in our thinking allows it to have its proper place in our lives so that we can live with wisdom.

Our reactive mind and our conditioning combine to cause anger. If we see or hear something that is very different from the way we think it should be, we can react with irritation or anger, depending on the situation. Examples here could include: if a child is doing something we regard as wrong, like smoking, or if your partner is not doing their share of the cooking at home. In some instances, before the feeling of anger, there is a feeling of being hurt or being mistreated. Examples here could include: if you criticise me, or if you have not done what you said you would, or if an airline cancels a flight and will not offer a refund. Sometimes we get angry with ourselves if something is not going the way we want: if we have not performed well enough in a test or if we made a wrong financial decision. In my medical career, I treated many young men who had punched a wall in anger and hurt themselves. The angry person is sure he/she is right, and the others are wrong. It is an unconscious process.

Some people are unable to control their anger, even if they would like to. This is because the reaction can be so explosive that it is difficult to stop. We rarely pause to consider the effect our anger is going to have on others. We are more likely to express our anger when we think the other person cannot harm us back: a child, a spouse, an employee, or when we are on the phone. At other times we internalise it, are seething with anger, but do not express it openly because we are worried about the repercussions.

As part of the Human Wisdom Project, I run small dialogue sessions with children and teachers in schools, and many children are brought up to believe that anger is a legitimate way of resolving a disagreement with someone and getting your own way. It is a form of violence in this context. What begins in the school playground continues on the streets. I ask them, "What would happen if you were an adult and punched someone you had an argument with?" "We would end up in jail", they would say. So many young men do exactly that because they have never been taught to understand their anger and manage it intelligently. Once the pattern of anger is established, it is tough to break. At one of the talks I was giving, I met a lady who said her husband had an anger problem and whenever he was angry, he would get abusive. Afterwards, he would calm down and be apologetic, but was unable to control his anger the next time he got upset. He went to anger management sessions to try and get the problem sorted, but his anger continued and they broke up.

Arguments can quickly spiral out of control resulting in anger and can damage our relationships. Our reactive mind can be easily triggered, feels hurt by what someone says or does, and we respond with anger and loss of self-control. We are more likely to respond with anger if we are already uneasy or agitated about something. All the minor irritations can add up to make us more easily provoked. It may be as a result of something that happened yesterday or a long time ago. The other person reacts to our tone, responds with anger, and a shouting match ensues, where nobody is listening. Each person loses control of their emotions. People dredge up hurts and arguments from the past as clubs to bash each other with, and it can get quite nasty. In the heat of such an argument, we say things which we may not mean to say, and that can cause incalculable harm. The anger can result in violence and is a pattern seen in many abusive relationships. Each person is absolutely convinced that they are right and the other person is wrong, and their self-righteousness fuels their anger further.

So, what can we do to avoid the many problems our anger can cause? Perhaps we need to explore its origins in our thinking and understand the nature of conditioning and the reactive mind.

Here are four questions we could ask when we see the first hint of anger rising in us:

- Is there another way of seeing this situation?
- Can I accept things as they are?
- Can I walk away and defer the conversation till later when I am calmer?
- If I do get angry, how will it be received, and how will the other person react?

These questions may allow us to respond to that feeling of anger in an enlightened way and avoid upsetting ourselves and others. Once we lose control and get angry, we have no idea of the repercussions of that for ourselves and others. Anger passes. If we can wait till it does, we can deal with the issues that need addressing in a much more constructive way.

A NEGATIVE ATTITUDE

Why are some people naturally negative in the way they see the world, and others much more positive? Which group are you in? What implications does this have for the stress we experience? Is it possible to change from one to the other?

Our attitudes are shaped by our conditioning. If we have had a tough life, where people have been mean to us, we will be naturally untrusting of the people we meet. This negative attitude affects us in different ways. We:

- Usually see the worst in people and their motives.
- Find it difficult to trust others.
- Are pessimistic and believe that the worst will happen (in all situations).
- Get upset easily.
- Can become paranoid, thinking that others are out to 'get us'.
- Often see threats where there are none.
- Become anxious about the future: our health, our children, our wealth, and so on.

All this happens unknowingly and is shaped by our past influences. Is it possible to change? The first step is to become aware of how our conditioning has shaped us. We may realise that we see people and the world as a threat, and we can explore the implications of this for ourselves. We realise that we often see threats where there are none, believe that people have behaved badly when they have not, imagine the worst will happen in the future when it does not, and so on. Just because one or two people have disappointed us, does not mean that everyone is the same. We may realise that this negative attitude does not serve us well, resulting in stress. Can we change? Awareness of this process without judgement brings understanding, and this can bring change. We could ask ourselves a simple question – is there a more positive way to see this situation? That question can open the door to a different perspective, and our attitude can change.

This does not mean that there are no threats in the world, or that people can always be trusted, or unfortunate things do not happen. People who are self-aware (or are working towards this) can accept this and yet move through the world with a positive attitude, seeing the best in people and situations. They do not believe that the worst is going to happen, and do not waste time worrying about the future. They experience much less stress and anxiety as a result. If we think the best of people, they are often inspired to be the best person they can be in response. If people do disappoint us, we need to accept that they too are shaped by their conditioning (like we are), and that they also act from their hidden self-interest, just as we do. If their actions succeeded in making us cynical and develop a negative mindset, they would have caused much more long-term harm than we realise.

Our memories of pain

Some people carry memories of the psychological pain they have experienced for many years. Others are able to leave them behind. Those memories continue to cause stress, long after the event is over. It is an unconscious process. What can we do to respond to these painful memories with intelligence?

Sorrow comes in many guises. It could be caused by abuse in childhood, an unhappy relationship, failure, loss of something we value, being physically attacked, and so on. People stop speaking to each other because of some past hurt. Friendships break up. People divorce and carry the pain of that for years.

These challenges are a part of all our lives. How do we respond? The incident may have occurred months or years ago, but why do we continue to suffer now? We hold on to the memory of that pain, or perhaps it holds on to us, and it continues to influence our life. None of us wants to live in pain, so how can we find a way to be free of the sorrows of our past?

They say that time heals all wounds, but life is short, so why wait?

The first step is to realise that the pain has conditioned us and shaped who we are, and find out the different ways it has done so. It may have made us bitter and angry. It may make us anxious about being hurt again, so we may not allow ourselves to be close to others, or we may be suspicious of people and their motives. Even though the pain occurred years ago, the memory of that stops us from being happy today.

The second step is to understand the nature of conditioning and our reactive mind, which we have discussed. It is an unconscious process. We react to the world from the content of our conditioning, including our memory of pain – usually in an automatic manner. We understand the mechanism by which the pain has conditioned us and why it continues to influence our lives.

If we feel that we have been wronged by others, and that has been painful, we find it hard to forgive them. We become attached to our narrative of what happened and repeat the story to whoever will listen, hoping to win their sympathies. Our sorrow is kept fresh by our thinking. We do not realise that others will have their own narrative of the same incident and they will also justify what happened.

Why do we struggle to let our painful memories go? Perhaps they strengthen the 'me' in subtle ways. It is 'my' suffering, it attracts sympathy, and I become attached to 'my' narrative. Whatever strengthens the 'me', brings pleasure. The pain, and my story of how it affected me, become part of my identity, and I do not want to let that go. We are not aware of this process, which is the same in all human beings.

If we see all this clearly, what can we do to change so that we may live freshly in the present and be free? We cannot turn the clock back and cannot erase the memory from our brains, so how can we respond? Being aware of the patterns of thinking that operate in the background means that they do not operate unconsciously anymore. This awakens an inner intelligence, which has the potential to bring change. Every time the painful memory arises in us, it is met by our intelligence, which sees the entire process clearly. Gradually its power fades away. We may let go of our attachment to our narrative of what happened, accepting that there may be other ways of seeing the same situation. We may find a way of forgiving the people who we think hurt us. As we begin to understand ourselves better, we see that our mind functions in the same way as everyone else's, and that can awaken compassion. We see that the behaviour of others is shaped by their conditioning and self-interest, and we are the same. Without an awareness of this process, neither of us can help our behaviour and actions, however much we think we are individuals in control of our lives. This does not absolve us of responsibility for our actions but does explain people's behaviour, including our own.

Initially, this awareness may be difficult to sustain over a long period. That is okay. The key is to begin, and just notice our thoughts and feelings when we can, and accept it when we cannot. With patience and perseverance, this ability to carry our awareness with us throughout the day improves. This awareness is alive when a painful memory is triggered (for example), and rather than reacting to it, we can watch it and allow it to pass, as we would a floating cloud.

We all have this capacity for acting from (or 'in concert with') our native intelligence, and if we can discover this naturally arising insight for ourselves by understanding ourselves deeply and the unconscious mechanisms which drive so much of human behaviour, we can live in freedom.

BEING VS. BECOMING

If we observe our thoughts, we will find that our mind is always buzzing, thinking of the next thing we need to do, and at the end of the day, our brain feels tired because the engine of thinking has had no rest. We are much more interested in the next thing that needs doing rather than being in the moment.

For some people, this process is stressful because they never manage to finish all the things they need to do, and that can make them feel inadequate. They think their happiness or satisfaction lies in the future, in getting all their jobs done, and since that always seems out of reach, they get stressed.

The machinery of thinking is always active, moving from one thing to the next and is never still. Many of us may find it difficult to stop, be still, and enjoy the moment we are in. When we are thinking about anything, we cannot be fully aware of our surroundings at the same time. We are only truly alive in the moment we are in, but if we are always thinking about the next thing to do, we cannot be present and savour the life we have, the one right in front of us, from one moment to the next. We think our happiness lies in some imagined future, but when the future arrives, it is not quite as we imagined it to be, whether it is a new suit or a relationship, and we are already thinking about the next goal to chase after.

Even if we are working, or listening to a concert performance, our mind wanders off, thinking of something else. Despite all the advances in technology, we are busier than ever. We think about things to do, or conversations we have had, or experiences we want to have, or what we are going to do to get ahead in life, and so on.

Thinking is essential for life, but it happens unconsciously and almost continuously, like an engine that never stops. We never leave a car engine running all the time, unless we need to travel somewhere, because otherwise it would wear out. Somehow, the engine of our thinking process is busy all day, even when it does not need to be. We do not seem to have any control over it. What would happen if we had a thought process that was active when it needed to be, but was able to quieten down when it was not? In this quietness, our senses are still awake, noticing what is happening. The mind is not asleep. This would allow us to notice things that we usually overlook, like the beauty of trees, or the magic of birds, or what people are not able to say.

Why is our thinking process so active when it does not need to be? There are, of course, things we need to do, but perhaps this constant activity is also a way of dealing with the ache of being still and doing nothing. Or the prospect of doing nothing. Thinking provides an easy distraction to being in the present. Our smartphones and other forms of entertainment offer other ways to distract ourselves. This process is the same in all human beings because our minds function in similar ways.

So how can we be more present in our own life? The first step is to become aware of this habit of thinking, of feeling uneasy, and the impulse to move away from the moment we are in. Gradually, as we are able to watch our mind without judgement, it becomes quiet. We can allow ourselves to relax and be fully present in the moment. Try it and see. It brings a sense of quietude and peace. All the essential things that need doing will still get done.

Children have this gift of being fully immersed in the present, but they tend to lose it as they grow up. If you watch them, they can be completely engrossed in whatever it is they are doing, and are able to listen with complete attention. Perhaps they have something important to teach us.

OUR OPINIONS AND BELIEFS ARE CHALLENGED

When our strongly held opinions or beliefs are challenged, we get stressed and can react with anger, as if we are being personally attacked.

Consider the example of the United Kingdom, which was divided on the issue of Brexit, with people holding strong views on both sides of the argument. If you challenged someone and presented a different perspective, they would get defensive and react with agitation and anger. A member of parliament in the UK was killed by a man who disagreed with her view on Brexit. Similarly, when strongly held religious beliefs are challenged, that can lead to a violent reaction. Or, if we are strongly patriotic and someone is critical of our country, it can create a similar response.

Why does this happen? There seems to be no interval between the challenge and the response, no gap, no space for awareness to present itself. The more opinions and beliefs we are attached to, the greater the chance for stress to be triggered when those views are challenged. This is the same in all human beings.

Where do our opinions and beliefs come from? I asked a college lecturer this question and he said that nobody had asked him that question before. We assume our views and our beliefs are our own and we become attached to them, but do not see that many come from our unconscious, conditioning influences. If you watch a particular TV news channel, you may develop certain political views which you will think are your own, not realising that they are a result of having watched that channel. You may meet someone who has a completely different view, and struggle to understand how they can have that view, not realising that they probably have different conditioning influences.

Why do we get so attached to some of our opinions and beliefs, and not to others? Probably because certain ones strengthen the sense of 'me' and become a part of our identity. Notice the subtle pleasure you experience when someone agrees with your opinion, or when someone shares your belief, and also notice the discomfort, irritation, or anger you feel when these opinions and beliefs are challenged.

We want to be with people who share our opinions and beliefs. We feel more secure, do not feel as lonely, and it can keep our mind occupied. If we become conscious of this process operating in the background, we can respond with intelligence.

That intelligence may allow us to see the problems associated with this attachment to our opinions, the stress it can generate, and how it divides us from people with different opinions. We could let go of our attachment to our opinions, and by being able to accommodate other points of view and explore them, this might inspire others to do the same. So much conflict in our lives and in the world is associated with this attachment we have to our opinions and beliefs. All of that could end with this understanding. Imagine that.

NOT FEELING WE CAN COPE

Let us revisit this example: in the same office, faced with the same workload, some people get stressed by the burden and feel that they cannot cope, while others seem to manage just fine and do not feel stressed at all.

Why is that and what does it reveal about the nature of stress?

We assume that our reaction is justified and correct, so it must be the workload or manager that is to blame for our stress. It seems clear that most of the time, it is not the workload itself, but our reaction to it that is causing our stress. What affects our ability to cope with situations? The question itself may feel threatening because it implies that something might be wrong with 'me' and I start feeling defensive. If we can put our reactions and judgements to one side and just explore the question out of curiosity, we may discover something new that may help us cope better with challenging situations, at home and at work.

Sometimes, it is not meeting the expectations of others which can make us feel stressed. For example, the manager may say that we must complete the work in an hour, and we take much longer. We are afraid of being told off. We may compare ourselves with our colleagues who are better than us at the same job and we feel inferior in some way. If we could take a step back and put our automatic reaction to one side, we could ask if there is a different way to respond. How could we improve what we are doing? We could explore the nature of fear and comparison, and that may provide new ways of responding. We could understand the subject of criticism and find a better way to deal with the situation. We may accept that everyone has different levels of ability and be happy with our own. We could speak to the manager about the workload. Or we may decide that this job is not suitable for us and find another one. All these different options open up for our consideration if we can step away from our initial stress reaction and explore the situation and our response from different perspectives.

At times, the pressure to conform comes from within us. We feel that the work should be done to a certain standard, and feel bad that we cannot do that, and get stressed. Stepping back may allow us to question our own ideals and ask if there is a different way of seeing the same situation. We may be putting ourselves under unnecessary pressure.

When faced with a big task, we may feel overwhelmed by the size of it. It could be hosting a dinner for a large number of people, or meeting a work deadline, or starting a new project, or moving to a new city or country for a job. How can we approach this in a fresh way? The first step is to ask ourselves how we can see things differently. It could be that we need to break the task down into many manageable jobs, create a plan, and then just begin. Once we begin, the path opens up and becomes clearer. For example, in writing this book, I did not know if I had enough material, or a clear idea of what shape it would take, or how it would be received. Once I began, the book just seemed to write itself. We often limit ourselves unnecessarily by thinking, "I am not capable of doing this", and that is the reason we get stressed. We human beings are enormously capable once we set our minds to something.

I think of running 5k, and I believe I will never be able to do that. I start running and manage that, but then think that I could never run a marathon. Once I start training, I find that I can manage that as well. And then I look at the people who run ultramarathons, and wonder how on earth they manage that! People run for 24 hours, with only two to three hours of rest in between. It is the same human body that is capable of extraordinary things. It requires a shift in our mindset from thinking of all the reasons why we cannot do something, to asking how we can. A positive attitude combined with some self-belief is all we sometimes need to get on and do the things that once seemed impossible. A simple question may make all the difference – "Is my thinking limiting me?"

WANTING MORE AND MORE

The human mind is never satisfied with what it has. It focuses on what it does not have and always wants more. More money, more experiences, more expensive holidays, more fame, a bigger house, or a bigger car.

Why are we so discontented? How much is enough?

We do not know contentment, so we do not know peace, and that is one reason why we get stressed. We put ourselves under enormous pressure to achieve, arrive, and get what we want, and run, run, run after our goals. We think that arriving at our destination will make us happy, only to be disappointed that the pleasure is short-lived, and so we find something else to run after. If we do not get what we want, we can get stressed.

Society applauds the person who runs farthest, accumulates the most, has the most power, and is the most famous. Without questioning it, we get conditioned by the society we grow up in to do the same. Everyone seems to want the same thing, so it becomes a competition, a race to the top. We never ask why we are running. We are probably just following all the people who are running. After all, they must know something we do not. In every race there is first the anxiety leading up to it, then the strain of the race itself, and then the huge disappointment that is experienced by the majority of people running because only a few people win. Even the winners find that their elation melts away quickly and they are left feeling empty again. People say that life is a race and only the fittest survive. That view needs to be challenged. There is enough on this earth for all of us, as long as we all learn to live with intelligence.

Overconsumption in the world is a major contributor to global warming. The richest 25% of the people on earth consume more than 75% of the world's resources. The core reason for this overconsumption lies within us because our minds are never satisfied and we continually want more and more for ourselves. More things and more experiences, all contribute to habituated overconsumption and global warming.

It is worth exploring why the human mind is never content and always wants more. The answer may not only help us be less stressed and live with a sense of peace, but also be great for the planet, and so ultimately for ourselves.

Three processes of thinking contribute to this phenomenon.

The first is conditioning. We are influenced by the environment we live in and most of us grow up accepting the values of that society, without questioning them for ourselves, with some exceptions of course. In this case, we never pause to ask why we want to spend all our energy and time accumulating more and more. Our life is a gift and our time on earth so short. Why waste it doing things we may not enjoy, knowing that the process has the potential to cause us anxiety and stress? Questioning our conditioning influences is an essential first step to understanding why we live the way we do. We could then ask such questions as: *How much is enough?*

The second process is the mind's unconscious search for pleasure and stimulation, which is an attempt to get away from its deep restless-ness and discontent. Pleasure is not wrong, but awareness allows us to respond to the search for pleasure with intelligence. Acquiring things and having positive experiences brings short-term gains. The pleasure quickly fades away, and sooner than later we feel empty and restless again. We need to repeat the pleasure, but this time it has to be bigger and better for us to experience the same sensation. This is what drives our need for more and more. We cannot think of a different way of being because this behaviour is ingrained in our thinking. Unquestioned. Unexamined. It is difficult for us to make that fateful but liberating connection between our search for pleasure and the stress we experience.

The third process is fear and insecurity. Our fear of the future and of not having enough drives us to accumulate more and more, 'just in case' we need it. Our fear and insecurity know no limit, so we never stop accumulating. These fears operate in the background, hidden from our awareness, so are never examined and never go away. They tend to exaggerate the negative, and so push us to work harder and harder to accumulate more and more. The millionaire wants their second million, the billionaire their second billion, and so on. Neither is ever content, despite having all that money. A mind that lives with fear, however subtle, knows no peace.

How can we respond to this understanding of the reasons behind our discontent with intelligence? It is too simplistic to say we should live without fear or without pleasure. That approach does not work because these patterns are deeply embedded in our thinking. Understanding them, however, can awaken our intelligence, which brings change. This journey towards understanding can require curiosity, passion, and perseverance, but is assured to lead to wisdom and will leave us with an enduring feeling of peace.

There is no need to be afraid of this process of enquiry. No one is demanding that we change or is going to take away anything we value. This enquiry is entirely up to us. If we look at our life and the state of the planet, we may ask if there is a different way to live – happily, with a sense of peace, and in harmony with ourselves, others, and the world. After all, none of us wants to live with anxiety, stress, disappointment, and heartache. A certain amount can propel us forward and is inevitable, but the useful distinction here is our long-term relationship with these experiences of our past. How we relate to them internally, and whether they drive us, or whether the most intelligent versions of ourselves are in charge.

We may realise that the drive to accumulate comes from within us. Without fear or judgement, we could begin to observe this process at work in ourselves, understanding its implications for our lives and the planet, and exploring the factors behind that.

In questioning our conditioning, we could explore the different ways in which we have been influenced by the society we live in. We could ask if it is in our interest, or is intelligent, to spend our lives chasing more and more, as we do. Is that what we want, or is it just something we picked up from our environment because everyone was doing the same thing? Just ask the question and see what emerges.

We could explore all the hidden ways our fears influence our lives. Once they come out of the shadows, we can examine them in the light of day and ask if they are real, how likely they are to happen, and if it is possible to live with intelligence.

Through this exploration, which awakens our intelligence, we would realise that we are beginning to change. This change occurs as part of our journey of enquiry to understand ourselves and how our minds work. The main focus remains on the enquiry, and change is just a by-product of that process. We could live in such a way that we had enough, with a sense of peace, free from the anxiety and stress caused by always wanting more, and in turn, we may just save the planet for future generations.

WHO SUFFERS?

"Who suffers?"

"I do."

"Who am I?"

What is the nature of the 'I' that experiences suffering?

In this section, I am going to leave you with some questions to ponder. They are at the core of being human. Perhaps in exploring them, you may discover something new. Of all the questions we may ask ourselves on this journey of enquiry, this is perhaps the most challenging because it has no ready answer. We may read what others have written on the subject, agree with them, and repeat what they have said to us and to others, but that brings no illumination. That understanding and the peace it brings, only come if we explore these questions for ourselves.

After exploring the external causes of our stress, and the origin of stress in ourselves, the third and perhaps most important question to ask is, "Who suffers?" We rarely ask this question. How is this 'I' that feels the stress put together? It feels real, like our physical body, but is it a mirage, created by our thinking?

The funny thing is when we try to find the 'I' inside ourselves, we cannot find it. Yet, the effects of the 'I' are there for us all to see. It is a strange phenomenon.

Why bother asking, "*Who suffers?*"

It is the 'I' which experiences all the stress, hurt, and suffering, so I am curious to find out what the 'I' is. Perhaps the answer may end my suffering altogether.

From the day I was born, I had a name that was unique to me and I looked uniquely different, as we all do. As I grew older, I accumulated all my experiences, and those memories became a part of me. I identified with those memories as 'me'. I also identified with my feelings, my possessions, my children, my job, my beliefs, my opinions, and my relationships, and they also became a part of 'me'. So, it is easy to see how the 'I' was created and how it feels unique.

It is more difficult to understand where our feelings come from. A clue lies in the fact that if you are feeling anxious about your job, for example, and you distract yourself by thinking about something else, your anxiety temporarily ends. As soon as you think about the job again, it comes back. This suggests that our feelings are linked to our thinking. Behind every emotion is a thought, though that is not easy to notice because our feelings arise so fast in us. I am referring here to feelings like desire, anger, fear, pleasure, and so on. If our feelings are a product of our thinking, and a part of the 'I', is it possible that the 'I' may also be a product of our thinking process?

Is the self a fixed entity? We know that we are different when we interact with different people. Each person brings out a different aspect of our personality. Having understood the nature of our conditioning and the reactive mind, each person we meet triggers a unique aspect of our memory, and we react from that. That is why we feel we are different with different people. We also change with time. As our conditioning changes and new experiences accumulate in our memory, we change.

If the self is not a fixed entity, is it created by our thinking? Could the self just be an identification with whatever thought or feeling emerges from our mind at that moment? Is there an 'I' separate from our thinking? Though the 'I' feels it is a separate and solid entity, it may be present only in the moment and linked to our thinking process.

If a disease like dementia or a stroke damages a part of my brain where my memories are stored, my personality changes, or I may lose my sense of who I am altogether. People around me do not recognise the person they see. This is another clue that my sense of self is linked to my thinking.

It is a beautiful autumn morning as I sit and write this. The morning sun casts long shadows onto the grass. There is a haze in the distance. Not a leaf stirs. It is so very still. Two squirrels chase each other up and down the garden, playing and going about their day, without care. The dewdrops on the grass glisten with light. A bird lands on the small water feature in the garden for a drink. As I watch all this, I also notice that within me, not a single thought stirs, and there is a deep quietness and sense of peace within. There is no sense of 'I' watching all this. It is quite beautiful.

Through my exploration, I have come to this point, where I see that it is the 'I' which gets stressed and suffers. Without the 'I' there would be no stress and no suffering. I also see tentatively that the 'I' may be a mirage created by my own thinking. It is easier to see the logic of it (intellectually) than to experience this as a truth.

Could we say that stress is a reaction from our memory to a particular event? Our memory is created by thinking, so it is a reaction from our thinking that creates stress. It may not be clear because it occurs so fast. If this is true, it follows that it is not possible for our thinking to 'solve' the problem of stress because the solution cannot come from the same place where the problem originated. If you are stressed about something, try as you will, your thinking cannot 'solve' this problem. The mind churns over the problem, going over what has happened, but that does not bring illumination or long-term freedom. If it is true that our stress is a reaction of our thinking to an event, it also follows that if we can meet the feeling of stress without thinking, it can ebb away. We will explore this later. This may come across as a strange idea because it may be new to you, but please keep an open mind and let us explore this together. Remember, it is only going to be true if you see it clearly for yourself.

Some questions have no easy answers, and the important thing is to stay with them and see what emerges, without any expectation. Asking, "Who suffers? Who am I?", is one of them. Try it, approach it with a playful curiosity, and find out what you discover. Do not be frightened by it. After all, it is only a question. The process is mysterious, beyond our conscious awareness, but just asking the question sometimes awakens an inner intelligence, and something within us may start shifting as a result.

THE NATURE OF STRESS

WATER HAS SIMILAR PROPERTIES NO matter where in the world it is found. Similarly, stress is also a process that has its own innate features, and there are certain facts about it that are the same in all human beings no matter what we do, how rich we are, or where we live. The feeling of stress and the mechanism behind it are the same, though the causes vary in each of us.

WE ARE NOT ALWAYS AWARE THAT WE ARE STRESSED

We know that stress results in the release of the hormone cortisol and that long-term stress can damage our physical and mental health. It is therefore crucial that we recognise when we are stressed so that we can do something about it.

Sometimes, we are not aware that we are stressed because it can manifest as physical symptoms which we may not associate with stress. Our sleep pattern may change, or we may get more frequent colds or other infections. Some people experience abdominal pain, or lose appetite, and may think that something is wrong with their gut. Or we may feel tired or irritable, or start drinking a bit more than usual. Some develop acne or an exacerbation of their eczema. Chest symptoms like palpitations or tightness in the chest can also be a result of stress.

A young woman once presented with low back pain. The MRI scan showed some mild degeneration, but nothing remarkable. I sent her for some physiotherapy, which did not help. I then tried some injections, which did not help either. I said that I did not know what else to do, and we should just wait. At her six-month review, she came in smiling and said her back pain had gone. I asked her if she had tried a new treatment. She said, "No, but as soon as I ended my stressful relationship, my back pain eased off".

Some people, particularly men, do not want to acknowledge their stress, whether to themselves or others. They may think that it is a sign of weakness, or are worried to have this on their medical record, or anxious what others will think about them.

Young people and children sometimes do not have the vocabulary to name their feelings as stress, and so, cannot make sense of them or describe them to others. Their stress expresses itself in their behaviour: a child who smashed everything in the class because she did not get the toy she wanted, or a boy who went and lay under the table for the entire session, or a girl who could not speak because of the traumas she had experienced.

When it comes to our health, and particularly mental health, our tendency is to deny that there is a problem as long as we can because we are worried about the consequences of acknowledging it. The earlier we can do it, the easier it is to deal with it, and either sort it out ourselves or get help.

WE LOSE OUR ABILITY TO THINK CLEARLY

Long-term stress is like a fire in the brain, and it can make us lose our ability to think clearly. Any strong emotion can do that. As a result, we can make bad decisions which can affect us adversely for years.

If we are stressed, many other emotions like fear or anger can be triggered as well. These emotions are powerful and can make us act in irrational ways.

I was once moving some blood vessels to one side to get access to a disc at the front of the spine. There was an accidental puncture of the common iliac vein, which is a major blood vessel, and the operative field quickly filled with blood. My stress levels were pretty high at this stage. There was the real possibility of losing the patient if I could not control and stop the bleeding. My instinct was to try and repair the blood vessel as best as I could, but I knew that that was not my area of expertise. I paused and considered the options. I knew where the bleeding had come from, so I just put my finger on the hole in the blood vessel, sucked up the excess blood, and asked the team to call for a vascular surgeon to come in and help me repair it. I knew that was the best chance the patient had. I stayed there for more than an hour, with my finger on the blood vessel. The vascular surgeon arrived, quickly repaired the tear, and all was fine with the patient. Doing the right thing in stressful situations is always a challenge because stress makes us lose our ability to think clearly.

We can see this in relationships wherein if you have an argument and get upset, your anger can make you lash out and say something nasty or even physically assault another person, without caring for the consequences. That can affect relationships for years if the injured survive the incident.

If I am sitting for an exam and come across a question that I do not know the answer to, I may get stressed, and this may affect my ability to think clearly about the rest of the paper.

Our stress can make us tell a lie, with unintended consequences. A politician was caught speeding by a traffic monitoring camera. To avoid a driving ban, he claimed that his wife was driving the car. The camera picked up that he was driving the vehicle, and he was prosecuted for perverting the cause of justice and went to jail. Or, we may tell what we may think is a small lie that will harm no one and because we believe we can get away with it. If we get caught out though, people conclude that we are not to be trusted, and that may damage our career – the small white lie having unintended consequences that we did not quite consider in our stress. It can be a real test of our integrity to own up to mistakes that we have made and accept the consequences. The temptation is to walk away, blame someone else, or cover up. Our fear and stress can make us do that. Since we stop thinking clearly, we do not do the right thing and suffer the consequences.

You could begin by noticing this inability to think clearly in small stressful situations. For example, when your partner asks you if you remembered to ring the plumber and you say, "Yes", when you have actually forgotten. Or, when you are lonely and a bit stressed, you may open a bottle of wine and drink it all, or overeat food that you know is not good for you.

Whenever we are stressed, it is, therefore, essential to recognise that our ability to think clearly is impaired. It is helpful to pause and explore other ways of seeing and responding to the same situation before deciding on an intelligent response. If you do this with small challenges, when the big ones arrive, you have been practising and are ready for them.

WE ZOOM IN AND LOSE PERSPECTIVE

If you fail an exam, 100% of your attention is focused on your failure. You may think that you are a failure and that your entire life is a failure and react to that.

If you are a doctor and a patient makes a serious complaint about you, you are suspended from work while this claim is being investigated. You may worry about your livelihood, what people and colleagues will think of you, and feel that your life as you know it has ended. You may think that your entire career is over and react to that.

If your partner leaves you for someone you know, you may zoom in on that, feel worthless and incapable of being loved, find yourself unable to face people, and react to that.

All three of the examples above are real stories of real people each of whom ended up taking their own life. In all these cases, each person had so much to be grateful for. Their health was excellent and they were loved by many people. But their stress caused their vision to narrow and they lost that perspective. Each one of them only saw failure and no way out.

If I have a pin in my finger, I zoom into that. The pain it is causing becomes the centre of my life. If my intelligence is operating, I can zoom out, see that it is just a pin in my finger, that the rest of me is okay, and take it out.

Why does our mind do that? Perhaps it is an evolutionary response from a time when physical threats were commonplace. By being able to focus on the problem, we could trigger the fight or flight response and protect ourselves. In the modern-day, we equate psychological threats to our sense of 'I' in the same way as a physical threat and respond in the same way. This can distort our thinking and lead us to zoom into a situation, whereas the intelligent response maybe to zoom out and see things in perspective. As we have discussed in an earlier section, it is worth exploring the question 'who suffers?', as this puts the whole sense of 'I' into perspective and offers us fresh ways of looking at the situation.

If we understand that the nature of stress is to make us zoom in and forget all the things that we still have to be thankful for, we can respond with intelligence.

STRESS MAKES US SELF-ABSORBED

If you have a toothache, all your attention is focused on the pain. It demands your attention. You cannot think of anything else or anybody else and you lose your sense of awareness of what is happening around you. Similarly, stress also makes us focus on the emotional pain we feel, and that can make us even more self-absorbed than normal.

How can being self-absorbed impact our lives?

If we are in a relationship and are thinking mainly about ourselves and our pain, we cannot be as loving or sensitive to the needs of others. This can strain all our relationships. We may not be able to pick up the signals from others as we are speaking to them, and that can cause difficulties in communication. Our expectation of others increases and we expect them to look after us, be sympathetic, and more caring. We talk about ourselves and our stress even more than we normally do, and look for people who will listen to us. We forget that others also have their needs. As a result, they could begin to find us tiring and not want to spend time with us. We are surprised when our friends drift away and do not understand why.

If we are thinking about ourselves and our pain, we become less sensitive to the beauty of the world and all the joys it offers us daily: the beauty of a bird in flight, or the laughter of a child, or a tree shining with light. If the pain we feel is severe, then we may withdraw from others and feel even more isolated and lonely.

When we wake up to this process going on behind the scenes and its potential to damage our relationships and cause us to withdraw from life, we can explore fresh ways of responding. We could put our own suffering to one side and become more aware of our surroundings and the beauty of the world. We could become better listeners and not just talk about our own problems that can become tiring for others. We could also become more interested in others and sensitive to their needs.

As a result of responding from this understanding, we could avoid becoming even more stressed than we already are, by not suffering the consequences of our increased self-absorption.

WE THINK THE CAUSE OF OUR STRESS IS 'OUT THERE'

If someone has not done something for me that they said they would, and I feel hurt, it is natural for me to feel that they are the cause of my pain and blame them for hurting me. Or, if I do not get on with some work colleagues, it is understandable for me to blame my job for my stress. Or if we are in a relationship, and you are not meeting my need to be understood, which I am not aware of, it follows that I think that you are the cause of my stress.

I feel certain that my perspective is correct because I have never learnt to doubt myself or explore whether the cause of the stress may lie within me.

The triggering event and my feeling of stress are so closely connected that it feels natural to assume that it is the event that is causing my stress. We try to change the other person or the situation, and if we cannot do that, we get even more frustrated and stressed. This cycle continues, as does our stress, and it can seem that there is no way out.

This is the instinctive way our mind responds, and it is not wrong. The main cause of our stress often lies in our reaction to an event from our unconscious patterns of thinking.

Questioning our immediate reaction and exploring other ways of seeing the same situation allows us to respond with intelligence.

Taking responsibility for how we feel is a challenge because we are so sure that the cause of our stress is 'out there' and because it is much easier to blame others for it. Because the feeling of stress arises in us, it follows that the root of it must be within us as well. If that is the case, this acceptance allows us to explore it and find out if we can end it in ourselves.

If I feel there is too much workload and I am stressed, I can explore that and realise that the main cause of my stress may be my fear of what others will think of me, my imagined fear of the consequences if I do not get the job done, or my idea of how much work I regard as acceptable. Or, I may think that the work should be done to a particular standard and am not willing to be flexible on that score. If I look around me, I can see that others may be doing the same work without getting stressed, and that may make me pause and ask why. If I am stressed in a relationship, my exploration may make me realise that the underlying cause of how I am feeling may lie in my own unmet emotional needs, which I am not aware of. I could take responsibility for these needs and discuss them with the other person, and that may lead to a solution.

OUR PATTERNS OF STRESS KEEP REPEATING THEMSELVES

If I get stressed being in a traffic jam, every time I am in one, I will get stressed. If I get stressed by an untidy house, I will keep getting stressed if the house is not tidy. If you do not like a particular person, each time you meet them, you will have the same reaction. My behavioural patterns also tend to repeat themselves. If my standard response to stress is to storm out of the room, bang doors, or sulk, then those patterns repeat themselves every time I am stressed. We are not aware that the patterns of stress keep repeating themselves in our lives, so we do not question what is happening.

We may have had an excellent education. No matter where we may have received our education, it most likely did not include an understanding of how our mind works. In other words, just because we are educated, does not mean that we have cultivated our inner intelligence. Such intelligence – innate to everyone – comes from self-understanding, and all of us are capable of discovering it. It is not an intellectual process, though it may seem like one.

If, on the other hand, we do not come to understand our unconscious thinking patterns of conditioning, comparison, and our reactive mind (as we have previously explored), we can understand why the patterns of stress keep repeating themselves in our lives. Our mind automatically compares what it sees with its unconscious conditioning, and anything that is very different from what we already know and expect can trigger a stress reaction, which is explosive and often unstoppable.

Because our unconscious conditioning remains unchanged, our reactions do not change either.

Our patterns of stress, fear, and pleasure repeat themselves in our lives. The paradox is that these patterns are much easier to spot in others than in ourselves, but we become defensive if anyone points them out to us. It is, therefore, worth asking ourselves, "What are the patterns of stress that recur in my life?", and write them down. We can then explore their origins in our thinking and see what we discover.

This is a living intelligence that operates from moment to moment. It is not something that can be discovered today and then used tomorrow. It emerges from seeing freshly, clearly, what is happening right now, and understanding the way our mind works.

If I notice that I am stressed by the same things repeatedly, I could ask why. Once a pattern is seen clearly and we understand its entire anatomy, there is the potential for a non-stress-induced response to step in, evaluate our current circumstance, and choose a different course of action than we might have taken in the past.

CONTROLLING OUR STRESS REACTION IS DIFFICULT

Stress is most often a reaction of our thinking to a person or event. The key word here is *reaction*. If we come across something that we do not like, the reaction is instant and can occasionally be explosive, depending on the circumstances. We do not see the thought process at work in the background and our first experience is of the stress that we feel. The trigger could be a thought, or being late for work, or an impending deadline.

Circumstances dictate how we express our stress. If we are afraid of the consequences, we may say nothing, but instead only internalise it. If we are not, we may get angry and shout at someone.

If we react with anger to our children looking at their mobile phones during dinner, that reaction is likely to repeat itself each time despite our efforts to control it. This is because of the nature of stress and the way our mind works, which is, as I have said before, the same in all human beings.

Because this stress reaction is automatic and sometimes explosive, the best way of managing it is to prevent it from triggering in the first place.

We think we should be able to control all our emotions and reactions, and most often we can modify the way we express them, but sometimes they are powerful and express themselves despite our best efforts to stop their expression. We may end up feeling guilty for getting angry, or get stressed, for example. If we understand the entire process behind these reactions, we could be less critical and kinder to ourselves.

If we cannot control our stress reaction, what can we do? There is a way to do that, but it is no quick-fix. It requires us to cultivate our inner intelligence, which comes from self-understanding, and we need to apply ourselves to that with passion, rigorously, and in a sustained way. The understanding does all the work.

TRYING 'NOT TO BE STRESSED' DOES NOT WORK

The most unhelpful thing you can tell someone who is stressed is "do not be stressed" or "be resilient". They may try and use their willpower to 'not to be stressed' but find that impossible, and do not know what to do. It seems a logical thing to say, but it does not help and does not work. On the contrary, it can increase the frustration a person feels because despite their best efforts, they are unable to end their own stress.

To understand why, we need to dig deeper into both, the process behind our stress reaction and the 'I' that wants to change it.

We have explored how stress is often a reaction of our unconscious conditioning to what we see or hear or think. If it is very different compared to what we regard as 'normal', or it threatens the 'I', we experience a disturbance in our thinking that we call stress. Though we do not see it because it occurs so fast, this reaction is a part of our thinking process. We seem to have little control over this reaction.

We have explored how the 'I' is also a product of our thinking. Where our thoughts are not active, there is no sense of 'I'. This can occur during deep sleep, or meditation, or just while looking at a bird in flight without a single thought arising. The 'I' is alive only in the moment we are in and is a thought which identifies with the content of our memory.

None of this is right or wrong, just something that each of us needs to explore and understand for ourselves. If for a moment, we accept that the above is true, though it may not be apparent, then it is understandable why the 'I' cannot solve the problem of my stress.

Stress is a response from our thinking and it cannot be solved by the 'I' that is also created by our thinking. In many cases, the 'I' is the cause of the problem. For example, when criticised, the 'I' feels threatened and reacts with stress.

While it is easy to manage a physical illness with medicines, it is much more difficult for our mind to solve the problem of stress, which comes from the same mind. This may explain why 70–80% of the people in many studies report being stressed. If it was easy to solve the problem, they would.

So, what can we do? We will use this understanding to explore how we can meet stress with intelligence. This intelligence is awakened when we become aware of the many processes of thinking that contribute to our stress.

HOW DO WE RESPOND TO STRESS?

OUR MIND RESPONDS TO STRESS in a range of predictable ways, which are similar in all human beings. Understanding these unconscious and automatic patterns of reaction to stress allows us to respond instead with intelligence and have more empathy for others. Not all of these apply to every person. There is some variability in our response based on our personality and other factors.

WE TRY TO CHANGE THINGS

If there is a pebble in my shoe, I will stop and take it out. That is common sense. If there is an obvious cause of my stress that is within my control, it is natural for me to do something about it. If I am stressed because I have a lot of things to do, I could make a list of jobs, prioritise, and just get on with doing them. If I have a toothache, I could see the dentist and get it sorted. If I play tennis and realise that I am not good enough because I am always losing, I could get some extra lessons and train harder. All these are common sense responses to stress.

There are, however, many areas where we have no control over the situation and continue to try and change things, resulting in increasing frustration and stress. If you have a different opinion to mine and I try and change it by arguing with you, you will just become defensive and argue back. I will keep repeating myself, persist with the argument, and we both end up stressed and frustrated. If I prefer organic food and you think that it is a waste of money, and I try to change your mind, we end up having an argument. If you support a right-wing political party and I support a left-wing party, we try to convince each other that we are right and conflict follows. Changing a flat tyre is much easier than changing someone's opinion.

It becomes apparent quite quickly that the only person we can change is ourselves. Trying to change another person's opinion, belief, or behaviour is challenging at best and often results in conflict and stress. This does not mean that we do not challenge prejudice and injustice, but we could do so with the understanding that most people are strongly attached to their point of view.

We also get stressed by many situations that are completely out of our control. These may include a cancelled flight, the loss of a job, or a financial loss. Accepting situations that cannot be changed, with all their consequences, is not easy, but is the intelligent thing to do. If we can do that, our stress begins to dissolve.

Whenever we are stressed, whether it is due to people or situations, our first instinct is to try and change things. It is worth pausing for a moment and asking if our intervention will make any difference. If not, we could instead focus on what needs to be done next.

BLAME OTHERS

When we are stressed, we look for someone to blame. If we lose our job, it is easy to blame the company for being responsible for it. If our friends do not invite us to a party, we may feel left out and blame them for ignoring us. If a train is cancelled because of bad weather, we blame the train company for our stress.

As we have explored before, the ultimate cause of our stress may lie within us because it is a reaction from our thinking to the world that we live in and the difference between how things are and how we want them to be. It could be our own unmet expectations that are causing our stress, or our sense of 'self' that is challenged, or if our inner needs are not met.

Sometimes there is no one to blame. Things just happen. Life is uncertain and it does not always go as per plan. Examples here could include a car accident resulting in a traffic jam, or an illness that forces me to cancel a trip. Even in these circumstances, we can look for someone to blame.

If someone we are close to disappoints us and does not do what they said they would, we can get upset and blame them for how we feel. We think that if they really loved us, they should have done that for us. What happens next? Most of the time, they will get defensive, justify their behaviour, get angry back at us, and the conflict grows. We could make them feel guilty for what they have done, but what does that achieve? We may feel like hurting them back for the pain we feel and that may make us feel good.

Blaming others for our stress prevents us from exploring the core reason for it in our thinking. As a result, the patterns of stress keep repeating themselves and the stress itself does not go away. If a colleague at work gets praised by my boss for some excellent work that they have done, and perhaps gets a bonus as a reward, I may feel bad and blame both, my boss and my colleague, for how I am feeling. I think I should also have been recognised for the work I do. That resentment grows over time. I would learn nothing from the stress I feel, think it is their fault, and that pattern would repeat itself. If instead, I paused, took responsibility, and asked myself what I could learn from that feeling, I would realise that it is the unconscious way my mind compares itself with others that is responsible for my stress. I would have learnt something new and could then explore that further.

There is a subtle pleasure in feeling that others are responsible for our pain. This is because it reinforces our sense of 'self'. We enjoy the sympathy we get from others and talking about what happened. It can make us feel like a victim, and once that pattern develops, that becomes our default reaction to life's adverse events. We never consider that people's behaviour towards us may have something to do with our own actions.

Each person responds in their own unique way to stress with different degrees of insight into what is happening. Blaming others is an instinctive response, but if we understand the process behind that, we may pause and allow our intelligence to respond instead.

GET ANGRY AND UPSET

Depending on the situation, our stress can make us angry and upset. If my colleague at work makes a complaint about me, I can get angry and stressed. That can make me want to retaliate and hurt them back. Conflict in our relationships can bring out the worst in us. It can degenerate into a war of attrition.

Sometimes there is no one to blame. I may have lost a pet. The grief I feel is very real and can take time to abate.

If I have failed an exam or done badly in an interview, I can get angry with myself.

This anger can make us behave irrationally, blind to the consequences of our actions. The root of this anger is our stress and psychological pain, though we often do not see that. All I can see is your behaviour which has made me angry and that makes me lash out at you.

We do not see the harm this anger does to our own health and the damage it does to our relationships. Staying with the hurt we feel, accepting responsibility for it, and exploring the beginnings of it in our thinking may allow us to respond with intelligence instead.

TRY AND ESCAPE

Stress feels like a fire in the brain and like all fires, our first instinct is to escape from it. This happens unconsciously, but has several unintended consequences that need to be understood. Many of these escapes compound the problem, damage our health, and adversely affect the lives of others. Understanding this allows us to deal with our stress differently, with wisdom.

The mind that feels stressed then tries to escape from the feeling, usually through pleasure. We never feel that we can avoid our stress but just 'deal' with it. We see others doing the same and this normalises our response.

Food is a common distraction from stress. Eating tasty food, going out to eat, and overeating, all bring a subtle pleasure and can result in obesity. As a result of stress, all our sense of control over how much we eat seems to disappear. This may explain why obesity rates are so high – 28% in the UK and 42.4% in the United States (2017–18). It is also a major cause of diabetes. We are not aware that we are overeating or that it may be a response to stress.

Obesity is a complex issue and there are many factors behind it including affordability of fresh food, our upbringing, whether we were taught to cook nutritious food, advertising, processed foods, hormonal imbalances, and so on. Living with inner intelligence means that we can make the best of our circumstances, of the cards that life has dealt us, and in which case, remain healthy. Living with intelligence also means that we move away from blaming others or ourselves for being obese, for example, and instead respond with empathy, kindness, and understanding.

We also escape through alcohol or drugs. Many people cite stress as the reason why they drink excessively, and the reason why they first started taking drugs, which can result in addiction. Both bring pleasure and can dull the emotional pain we feel. These addictions create new problems, which are worse than the original stressful event. Any addiction damages our relationships and we may find ourselves alone, and this aggravates our stress. We may lose our jobs and struggle to find another one. The pressure to escape is so powerful that it overrules any thought that warns us of danger. Since the stress has not been dealt with or understood, it does not go away. Even if the original stress begins to fade, we have by now become addicted and cannot go back.

In 2016–17, 8.5% of the adults in the UK between 16 and 59 had taken an illicit drug in the last year, and in 2017–18, 7.2% of all hospital admissions were linked to alcohol. In 2013, 9.4% of the population in the United States had used an illicit drug in the previous month. In 2015, 6.2% of the adults in the United States had an Alcohol Use Disorder, which is another way of saying that they had problems with drinking.

Why does the human mind that is otherwise so capable, act in a way that it knows is harmful to its health, and not be able to help it? The reason may be this unconscious response of using alcohol or drugs to escape from the feeling of stress.

Other forms of pleasure also offer a distraction from stress: shopping, watching television, our smartphones, and new hobbies.

In the right circumstances, some distraction may be the best way to deal with our immediate stress. Our inner intelligence, when active in us, can help us decide what is the right thing to do.

Escaping from any problem never solves it. In the midst of any crisis, it is very difficult for the mind to find a way out because we lose the ability to think clearly and stress reduces our ability to cope. We also find it difficult to listen to others who may be trying to help us because the compulsion to continue escaping is so strong. It is in times of crisis that our inner intelligence is most needed to steer a path through it without resorting to a form of escape that may damage our long-term health.

RUMINATE AND ANALYSE

If you have said something to me which has hurt my feelings, I will likely keep thinking over what happened. Whatever the cause of stress, the response is similar: thinking over what has happened, and playing the tape of that over and over in our mind. It is an unconscious and automatic process. It is the mind's way of trying to find a solution to the problem, but as we have discussed, that is not always easy (or effective) because many of our problems are caused *by* our thinking process. The more we think about an offence, the more our stress continues to affect us because all that recursive thinking keeps the memory of the past hurt alive. Sometimes this rumination over what has affected us and caused such a disturbance, manifests in our dreams.

As we ruminate over what has happened or what could happen, our stress continues. This process – our mind's attempt to resolve the pain – does not result in freedom. It is like a tiger going around in circles in its cage, looking for an escape, getting increasingly frustrated at not finding one. We are going to explore how changing our perspective and exploring the origins of stress in our thinking can end such vicious cycles completely.

GET DEPRESSED AND ANXIOUS

Long-term stress can be a trigger for both depression and anxiety, though other factors can also be responsible and our understanding is incomplete.

Symptoms of depression include a loss of enjoyment in normal activities, sleep disturbance, feeling worthless, loss of libido, lack of energy, angry outbursts, trouble concentrating, unexplained physical symptoms, and thoughts of suicide. Besides a stressful event, depression can also occur without an obvious cause because of thyroid problems, as a result of certain medicines, genetic factors, and substance abuse.

Symptoms of anxiety include excessive worrying, restlessness, feeling agitated, tense muscles, difficulty in sleeping, fatigue, difficulty in concentrating, irritability, panic attacks, and having irrational fears. Though stress is a major cause of anxiety, it can also be caused by some psychiatric drugs, substance abuse, as well as a response to physical health problems.

In the United States, about 18% of the population suffers from an anxiety disorder and 6.7% from a depressive disorder, though some suffer from both.

It follows that if we can find ways to both avoid stress and respond intelligently to it, we can avoid getting depressed or anxious. If we live with inner intelligence, which is awakened when we continue to work towards a better understanding of ourselves and how our minds work, we can remain mentally healthy.

WE FIND IT DIFFICULT TO TALK ABOUT OUR STRESS

Why do so many of us struggle to acknowledge to ourselves that we are stressed, depressed, or anxious, and struggle even more with the prospect of talking to others about our anxious states? What others think of us is often a concern and we worry that we will be looked upon as weak or inferior or that we will lose respect. If we are in a position of authority, we may feel that talking about our distress may undermine our position. There are few lonelier places to be than the head of a department or organisation. Men find it particularly challenging to talk about stress because they have more of a macho image to live up to. This comes from their unconscious conditioning.

Consider a scenario involving two people who live together. Let us call them Jack and Diana. Jack lost his job a few months ago and is at home. His partner Diana goes to work. He has worked all his life. He misses his friends at work, feels bad that he is no longer the bread winner in the family, and is anxious about the future. The power balance in their relationship starts subtly shifting. Diana expects him to do much more around the house and cook the evening meal, now that he is at home. He is not used to doing that. He starts feeling stressed but does not know how to deal with these feelings. He feels he should be able to sort it out himself but is unable to do so. The stress gets worse and he becomes withdrawn. Diana is worried about him and his mood swings start affecting their relationship. Jack has never opened up about his feelings to anyone before and is not sure how Diana will respond if he does. He worries if she knew how he was really feeling, she may lose interest in him and move on. His stress continues and their relationship gets strained, adding to his distress.

Accepting that we are stressed and talking about it can make us feel vulnerable and anxious as to how others will respond. Our relationships may be quite superficial and we are unsure if the other person will be interested enough to listen without jumping to conclusions. It is not that we do not want the problem resolved, but we may feel the need to be listened to deeply first. Even in our closest relationships, we may not feel that we will be understood and remain concerned about how it will affect the relationship.

All these reasons and more, keep us from being open about how we are feeling and sharing it with others. As a result, we continue to suffer quietly, unable to resolve the problem, unable to speak to someone, and anxious about getting help. We feel trapped within the walls of our suffering and our fear of sharing it with others. So, what can we do?

It may help to realise that we are not alone. Up to 80% of the population suffers from stress at some point in the year. We may think our stress is unique to us, but it is the same in all human beings. Sometimes, just speaking about our problems can be enough to resolve them and allow us to see them from a different perspective. If that does not resolve it, it is important to get help. The risk of not doing so is that the problem may get worse, be much more difficult to resolve, and lead us to possibly harm ourselves.

Self-harm

People can harm themselves as a response to stress. Psychologists say that people self-harm as a way of coping with their stress, of expressing their anguish, of getting attention and help, to punish themselves, or relieve unbearable tension. Often the person has no idea why they started doing it. Our social conditioning may play a role. Headteachers whom I speak to say it was rare 30 years ago, but most young people now are aware of it as a phenomenon and can get subtly conditioned to regard it as a way of expressing their anguish.

After giving a talk at a secondary school in England, I was saddened to hear that self-harm was common, particularly among girls, who were using blades from pencil sharpeners to do this. I met a young girl who was cutting herself, and she had no idea why she was doing so. She denied any emotional distress and her mother could not understand it either. More than half of the people who commit suicide have a history of self-harm. Focusing our energies on this group may prevent further tragedy later on.

Whatever the reason behind it, it can be prevented by an understanding of the roots of stress in our thinking and by learning intelligent ways to respond when it occurs.

SUICIDE

Suicide is an extreme act in response to an extreme degree of stress. The human instinct for self-preservation is so strong that anything that can override it must be even more powerful. The World Health Organization estimates that globally, 800,000 people a year take their own lives, and 20 times as many people attempt to do so. Young people account for a third of suicides globally. Every death and attempted suicide are a tragedy for both, the person suffering and their loved ones. The inner suffering of a person who is considering suicide is unimaginable. The person who attempts suicide feels there is no end to their particular problem and is unable to cope with the emotional distress it causes. It is not the person's 'fault'. The human mind functions in the same way in all of us. If we had the same conditioning influences and had to deal with the same challenges in life as those who make such a radical choice, we may respond in similar ways too. We need to move away from thinking it is 'right' or 'wrong' and instead treat people with compassion, which comes naturally when we realise that deep down, we are all the same. We are all human beings.

The causes of suicide are many. Common ones include poverty, job loss, grief, failure, relationship problems, mental health problems (like depression and anxiety), substance abuse, and a previous history of self-harm.

Even more alarmingly, the number of people committing suicide is on the rise in certain countries – between 2017 and 2019, the UK saw a rise of 25%. And in the United States, the number of suicides increased by 30% between the years 2000 and 2016. In other countries suicide rates are dropping.

Suicide can occur as an impulsive response to a stressful situation. As we have explored, stress makes us zoom in and lose perspective. It also makes us lose our ability to think clearly and in response to an extreme event, people can see no way out.

Suicide can also occur years after a stressful event. If people respond by taking to alcohol or drugs, that erodes their ability to cope and think clearly, and a downward spiral of addiction and health problems begins.

If this understanding of the way our minds work can be a part of education, many suicides could be prevented. For example, if we can learn to zoom out when faced with any crisis, that immediately puts it in perspective. We can appreciate that the rest of our life may be okay and we have many things to be grateful for. If we fail an exam, we can take it again. If someone we love leaves us, there will be other relationships that will follow. If there is a complaint against me, it will eventually pass. If I lose my job, I will find another one. Human beings have endured so many crises throughout history, and we can do the same. In the end, everything passes. Life moves on. What may seem like an unbearable stress today will be forgotten years later. In the midst of a crisis, it is our inner intelligence that is most needed – to allow us to put things in perspective, be grateful for what we already have, remind us that this storm will pass, and focus on what needs to be done next. As Robert Frost said in a poem in 1915, "The only way out is always through", meaning that we need to the face the challenges that life presents us with, and we can do that so much more ably when our inner intelligence is activated.

How can we bring this understanding to people who need it most? How can we help people who do not even know that they need it and who may even be resistant to receiving it? Each society needs to address this based on its unique circumstances, but I would suggest we begin with all children in education, not as a 'suicide prevention lecture', but much more broadly by integrating self-understanding into education. So many lives could be saved as a result.

This story is in the public domain, but touched me directly. A medical colleague I had worked with for many years took his own life a couple of years ago. He was one of the most conscientious and stable people one could meet. There was no history of mental illness in the past and he had a happy family life. One day he received a letter that a patient had filed a serious complaint against him and the police were also involved. The Medical Council opened an investigation into his conduct. He was suspended from work pending an investigation. At the inquest, his wife said that he feared his reputation would be in tatters and that the case would drag on for years. She had no clue that he had suicidal thoughts. One day he jumped off a bridge.

This story brought home to me the vital importance of living with this inner intelligence. None of us are immune to life's challenges, which can arrive at any time. We have no idea how we will cope because we have not been tested. This intelligence can help us respond in the most appropriate way and may even save our life.

HOW CAN WE AVOID STRESS?

Can stress be avoided or is it inevitable? We know that acute stress may be good for us because it makes us more alert and capable of dealing with the challenge in front of us. Some argue that it shapes our character and makes us resilient. Chronic or long-term stress can, however, cause serious mental and physical health problems.

We can use our understanding of the way our mind works to avoid much of the stress we experience in our lives. We could avoid it completely in some situations or it could reduce and become much more manageable. We have to give our passion to this, using all the skills introduced in previous chapters. Our lives could transform as a result.

Understand our conditioning

As we have explored, so much of our stress is a reaction from our conditioning to the world around us. We are usually not aware that we have been conditioned by all our experiences and influences. Our mind is constantly comparing what it receives through the senses with what it regards as 'normal', and if it is different, it can create a disturbance that we call stress.

We could begin by realising that we have been conditioned by our past, without our awareness or consent. It is not wrong, just the way the human mind works. We could then observe how this expresses itself through our opinions, beliefs, aspirations, and behaviour. The next step is to question our conditioning, understand where it came from, and ask what the intelligent response is.

Observe how this conditioning contributes to our stress. The next time you feel stressed, explore the roots of it in your conditioning. You may find that your stress is just a difference between how things are and how you want them to be. We think the problem lies in how things are. Could our stress be caused by our attachment to how we want things to be, which comes from our unexamined conditioning?

Consider this example. I may have grown up in a country where women did all the housework and I saw my mother do the same. I got conditioned by that and it became my opinion and my norm, but I was unaware of this. You, on the other hand, grew up in a different country, and in your home, men shared the housework equally and that became your norm. When we started living together, there was a conflict because I felt that you should do the cooking and run the house and you felt that I should do my equal share of it. I kept insisting that I was right and put subtle pressure on you to change. This conflict carried on for years. One day when I asked myself where do my opinions come from and why I was attached to them, I realised that I had been conditioned that way. I had never questioned my conditioning influences, but just assumed that they were right. It was as if a light went on in a room and I could see it all clearly. There was, of course, no logical reason why women should do all the cooking and housework out of obligation, and the conflict resolved completely.

The interesting thing is that the conflict resolved by seeing something clearly, not from an external pressure to change or even from an ideal to live up to.

Sometimes our negative experiences as children condition us to experience stress as adults. For example, if I grew up in a home where the adults were regularly uncaring, critical, or angry with me, I may get conditioned to think that the world is full of threats and I must remain vigilant. This makes me hypersensitive and much more prone to stress. I see threats where there are none and imagine the worst-case scenario. I tend to overreact. If I can explore the nature of conditioning and see how it plays out in my life, the unconscious effect it has on my behaviour ceases and I can be free.

The way social media causes stress is a good example to illustrate the power of unconscious conditioning. A young lady I met in a college said to me that the main cause of her stress was her eyebrows. Before you chuckle, do remember the same process that causes her stress, operates in you as well. She has been conditioned by social media to think that there is a perfect shape to an eyebrow and she then tries to copy that. If she cannot, it creates stress, which is the difference between how she is and how she wants to be. If we can be aware that the media unconsciously conditions us to create these images we want to aspire to, we can learn to accept ourselves as we are and our stress can be avoided or dissolved.

Our beliefs, which we unconsciously pick up from the culture we grow up in, can contribute to our stress. If I grow up in India, I am aware of the entire history of its conflict with Pakistan and may grow up disliking all Pakistanis. If I grow up in Pakistan, I may have the same feeling towards Indians, and feel threatened by them. If people from India and Pakistan meet, their unconscious conditioning plays out and there is conflict. The same is true for Catholics and Protestants in Ireland, or Shias and Sunnis in the Middle East, or Israelis and Palestinians. If I hold a particular belief and I meet someone who has a different belief, I can feel challenged and get stressed without understanding why. If we can wake up and understand that the same hidden process of conditioning is playing out in both of us, there is the potential for conflict to end.

If I grow up in a culture where drinking alcohol is banned, I will have an adverse reaction to people who drink regularly. If I can use discernment to question my rigid perspective, I may realise that it is not an original view anyway since my opinions come from the society I grew up in. I may accept that how adults behave is entirely their business and that people are different. As a result, my stress around this issue goes away. This approach also allows me to accept other people as they are because they too have been shaped by their conditioning influences and are likely not aware of their conditioned inner processes either – and in that respect, are similar to me.

Questioning our conditioning is not easy and if we have never done so before, it can feel strange. It is, however, one of the central doorways to our inner intelligence.

To begin this kind of dialogue with yourself, try this exercise: sit down with a notebook and write – *How does my conditioning influence my opinions, behaviours, and beliefs, and contribute to my stress?* Then write down what arises in response. Or, observe your stress reaction and trace its roots in your conditioning. This is a dynamic process, from moment to moment – observing, accepting, and then questioning where thoughts and feelings originate. If I question your behaviour, there is likely to be resistance. If you can question yourself, there is likely to be little or no resistance. The key thing to remember is that as far as this enquiry is concerned, there is no right or wrong.

LEARN FROM OUR REACTIONS

The intelligent mind has discernment and is always curious and open to learning about itself, and there is no better way to do this than by studying our reactions. Stress can change from a problem to be solved to an occasion for learning about ourselves. This can awaken in us an inner intelligence, which can help us avoid and overcome stress.

We have explored how the human mind is reactive. We do not know when a reaction will be triggered or how powerful it will be. These reactions could be minor or explosive, and we often have little control over them arising in us, though we are most often able to control how they are expressed. They follow a familiar pattern and we respond in predictable ways to the same trigger. Our immediate and understandable response is to be sure that our reaction is justified and to blame the other person or situation for causing our stress. Because these reactions emerge from our unconscious conditioning, when dispassionately observed, they can provide valuable insights into what is going on in our inner spaces.

What can I learn from my reactions? It is a beautiful question that opens the door to further enquiry and wisdom. It is also one that we rarely ask ourselves. Ask, and see what emerges. We could begin by observing our reactions usually after they have occurred. The second step is to accept them as they are and not judge them as right or wrong because any judgement blocks further enquiry. The third step is the most important. We could then ask where they come from and what they reveal about our unconscious conditioning and our patterns of thinking. That opens the door to intelligence.

You can see this in action in how we react to the people we know. We often have predictable reactions to the same people. Sometimes the mention of certain people evokes a strong negative response and that same feeling strikes within us each time the thought of them arises. We do not see that our reactions emerge from our *memory* of them and not the person as he or she is today – perhaps standing right in front of us. So often, we make sweeping judgements of people based upon a few memories. They could have changed and they may no longer be the people we once knew. Our initial judgement could also be mistaken. This understanding allows us to view people with compassion, accept them as they are, and look for the best in them. Very few people act from malice, just from ignorance based upon their own conditioning, which largely controls their thoughts and actions. Self-understanding awakens intelligence, which leads to empathy and compassion and allows us to move from a reactive approach to life to one where we can respond with wisdom.

We can learn about our prejudices from our reactions. We first have to accept that we all probably have some. Our prejudices are a result of an unconscious process, comparing what we see with our conditioning. Any difference we find creates a disturbance that can manifest as a prejudice. Once the unconscious is made conscious by our awareness, our intelligence is awakened and our prejudices can steadily disappear. We may dislike and have negative opinions about gay people or Jews or Muslims or immigrants or people from a particular country, and so on. If we can observe our reactions, notice our prejudices, and explore their roots, we will find that they have their origins in our unconscious conditioning influences. These could include the opinions of the people we grew up with, social media, newspapers we may read, or our own negative experiences. Our mind tends to generalise, therefore, a few people belonging to one community that does something that we do not like may make us think that everyone from that community is the same. We can ask ourselves if that is an intelligent perspective to be attached to. This exploration can bring freedom from our prejudices. This is a tremendous freedom, like a huge weight being lifted off our shoulders.

Our reactions reveal our images of ourselves. If I am a dancer and you are not complimentary about a performance that I have given, I will get upset. If on the other hand, you do not praise my cooking, I may just laugh and agree with you. If the images I have of myself are challenged, in this case of being a good dancer, then I experience stress. I may not even be aware of these images until the reaction occurs.

Our expectations of others are also revealed through our reactions. It is only when we react with hurt to a situation that we realise that we were harbouring an expectation in the first place. Examples here could be if my friend does not remember to come for a play that I was acting in or if I am not recognised for my contributions at work. When I react and feel hurt, I can ask what was behind that, and it is often an unmet expectation. I can then explore all my expectations, ask where they come from, and examine them using my intelligence. Since these expectations arise most often in our closest relationships, exploring them with the people closest to us can help us uncover them more fully. This dialogue is not easy at first. You could begin by saying that you accept that your expectations are your responsibility and you do not blame the other person in any way for not meeting them. That may allow the other person to be equally open. These expectations then no longer act unconsciously in the background. We realise that the more expectations we have, the more the chances of our getting hurt and angry when they are not met. This does not mean that expectations are bad and we should not have any. We are just exploring the subject to see what we can learn.

The 'volume' or extent of our reactions vary. It is the small 'low-volume' reactions that we really need to be sensitive to and watch out for because they can go unnoticed and influence our lives in subtle ways. This is how our unconscious fears operate to limit our lives and make us prisoners of our conditioning. For example, if we are afraid of conflict, we will not discuss a problem that is bothering us in our relationship, allowing it to get worse until it becomes a major issue. Or, our fear of change may make us put up with an abusive relationship or a bad job. Waking up to these 'low-volume' and subtle reactions that occur every day allows us to examine their roots in our thinking, learn something about ourselves, and that awakens intelligence.

The other advantage of noticing and learning from our reactions is that we are eventually able to spot the reactions as they are occurring and we can meet them with intelligence. That can change our automatic response to one which is considered and intelligent.

All this begins with a simple yet powerful question, "What can I learn from my reactions?" Write it down in your journal. Sit with it and see what emerges in response. That is the beginning of the journey of enquiry.

UNDERSTAND OUR IMAGES AND LET THEM GO

We carry with us so many images or opinions of ourselves and others, often without realising it. We have explored earlier how our images can be a cause of our own stress if others do not acknowledge or reinforce them or if they are challenged in any way. The more images or opinions we have of ourselves, the more the chance that we will get stressed. We also have many images of others, which are shaped by our memories of them. Our images of others can act as a barrier and can block meaningful connections or result in conflict. If the image I have of myself or others is different from the fact, then that can cause stress.

We could question why we need to have any images anyway. What purpose do they serve? Do they enhance our lives in some way? Yes, they can bring pleasure when they are reinforced, but as with all pleasure, the other side of that coin is pain. Leaving pleasure aside, do they serve any other purpose? Or, can they get in the way of accepting ourselves as we are, and seeing others freshly?

All our images of ourselves and others become woven into our sense of identity, and that is another reason why we are attached to them. Again, these images arise from our unconscious conditioning and from our experiences. Other people are often nothing like the images we have of them. I once met a well-known politician and realised that he was nothing like the image I carried of all politicians as being shallow and self-serving. These images had accrued over the years from media stories about scandals involving politicians in general. The person I met worked hard, was dedicated to the people he served, and wanted to make a difference, with passion. We became, and I am happy to say, are still friends.

Another example could be of a young man who thinks that he is 'cool' and works to create that persona for himself by how he dresses, what he does, the books he reads, and the music he listens to. He does that to be liked by others and make an impression. He starts posting stories of his thoughts and what he is doing on social media, in the hope that he will get many 'likes' from others. He is not aware that he is doing this. He finds that other friends are getting many more 'likes' for their posts than he is and begins to get stressed as a result. He spends all his spare time on social media, burnishing his image, trying to get more 'likes', and his frustration and disappointment increases.

How can we begin to understand our many images and then let them go?

The first step is to observe the images we do have of ourselves and others, without judgement. It needs a certain level of humility to look at our opinions and realise that they may not be accurate. Questioning them is the first step to responding with intelligence. We could also invite feedback from our closest friends about how they see us and we may be surprised that their perception of us is nothing like our own or the one we expected to hear. Once we have noticed these images in action, we can explore their roots in our conditioning. How did we acquire them? Why have they so embedded themselves into our thinking? Were they reinforced when someone called me a 'good public speaker', bringing a subtle pleasure, which I wanted to repeat? I did not consciously decide to have them. They all seeped into my thinking uninvited and without my awareness.

As we have discussed, this process of looking and understanding is not an intellectual affair. Can we notice and be aware of what is happening, and do so without language? As we have explored, this means noticing our images without labelling them as good or bad, right or wrong, but instead just observing them in action, seeing how they operate within us, and how they shape our lives.

You may say, "I have tried that and I am no different, so now, what am I to do?" There is no method or magic formula I can give you. This journey of enquiry into our inner spaces needs passion, curiosity, and perseverance. Suddenly, one day you will wake up and find that you are changed. All you need to do is to keep looking, learning, and questioning. Give it your heart!

In the course of my previous career, I realised that I had developed an image of myself as a good spine surgeon. I can see how it began to form without my conscious awareness. When patients did well after surgery, they would say nice things, or give a card, and that brought pleasure. I would share that with others close to me and that brought more pleasure when they said, "Well done". I would want others to acknowledge that image when I met them or would try and get that image reinforced in other ways. If the image was ever challenged – for example, if there was a complaint – I got quite stressed. I would also get stressed if my colleagues did not acknowledge that I was an excellent surgeon. All this happened subtly behind the screen of my awareness. Once I realised what was happening and the way it was affecting my life, I was able to just let that image go. I still carried on doing the same work, but with a much greater sense of freedom because the energy to keep that image alive was no longer needed and the stress associated with it also disappeared. This example also made me realise that pleasure and pain are two sides of the same coin. Whatever brings pleasure can also bring pain, in this case, my image of being a good surgeon.

The difference between who we are and our hidden images of who we want to be can create stress and disappointment. If I am unable to accept myself as I am, for example, and want to be a different body shape, I may start taking anabolic steroids, become ill, and not under-stand why. Waking up to these images we have of ourselves allows us to question them, and once we see the effect they have on our life, we can let them go. This may also allow us to accept ourselves as we are, with compassion, and be comfortable in our own skin, which brings such tremendous freedom.

The same process applies to our images of others. In college, there was a person who I felt was very annoying. This continued throughout our time together and we just avoided each other. We met through mutual friends more than 20 years later and I realised that I still carried negative images of him from all those years ago. This was subtle and in the background. As soon as I became aware of this, I realised that this was not intelligent, and I was able to let those images go and met him freshly. We had a wonderful time.

Can we meet people freshly, putting old images of them to one side? If we have negative images of them, we see them through the screen of that memory without realising it. The other person senses that and responds in a similar way. If we can meet others freshly, without the images of our past, a lot of potential stress can be avoided.

Letting go of our images of ourselves and others is not difficult once we become aware of them and see how they operate in the background, influencing our lives in subtle ways, including being responsible for our stress. I know some of them are woven into our identity, our sense of who we are, and it seems harder to let them go. Our identity, like the 'I', is a creation of our thinking, a mirage of our own making. Once we see that, letting go of these images is not difficult, and brings tremendous freedom.

The question that always opens the door to wisdom is, "How can I respond with intelligence to the role my images play in shaping my life?"

QUESTION WHY WE WANT TO BE IMPORTANT

The need to feel important is part of how the human mind functions. We usually do not question it because we are not aware of it. It operates from behind the screen of our awareness. What is wrong with wanting to be important? It brings pleasure and makes us happy. Surely that must be a good thing? Our society recognises merit and gives out so many awards – all sport is built on this, as are the awards that the governments give out to individuals. Soldiers are given medals. What is wrong with that? To explore and understand ourselves, we need to move away from the 'right' or 'wrong' approach and put that to one side. We could just explore how this impacts our life, and the different ways it can cause stress.

The need to be recognised and feel important is powerful. I was exploring this with some teachers in a school. They said it is like saying to the headteacher, "Here are the keys to my happiness. Please make me feel important and that will make me happy. If the head does not make me feel important, I will be unhappy, stressed, or angry, and blame them for it". The entire process operates unconsciously. The only bit we are aware of is that we may glow with pride when we are made to feel important and feel stressed when we are not.

I was once lecturing a group of doctors, and at the end, one of them said, "I am really stressed because no one at work recognises my worth and I do not know what to do about it. It is burning me up". Why do we need others to recognise our worth or say that we are doing a good job? Can we value ourselves and the work we are doing? As soon as we have an expectation that others should make us feel important, we open ourselves to getting hurt and becoming stressed.

In all organisations, human beings vie to be important. So many titles and hierarchies are created just for this purpose. As people jostle for recognition and importance, this sets in motion dynamics that generate disharmony between people. In the process, valuable energy is wasted, which could have been put to much better use.

An industry has arisen to give out 'awards' in every section of society. Many of them can be purchased for a price. I recall many years ago getting a letter saying that I had been chosen to have my name printed in a forthcoming 'Who's who' book. I would just have to pay a few hundred dollars for the book. My initial reaction was to glow with pride. I initially thought that I had been chosen by a panel until I realised it was a scam, which so many of us fall for, blinded by our need for recognition.

Behind the need to be recognised is a feeling that I want to be 'somebody'. The alternative is that I will be a 'nobody' and that makes us feel uncomfortable. We are powerfully conditioned by society to believe that being famous, respected by others, and wealthy are life's goals, and if I cannot be 'somebody', I will think that my life has been a failure. This is a construct of thinking created entirely by our conditioning and our need for pleasure. It needs to be examined, so that we can explore it and make our own mind up.

Being important, being 'somebody' brings pleasure and satisfaction, though it is short-lived. This deep-seated need for pleasure comes from our feeling of emptiness and the ache it creates in us. Our pleasures cover this ache for a while, but this emptiness never goes away and returns as soon as the pleasure recedes. As we have discussed, all pleasure is fleeting, and no matter how famous and important you are, the ache of emptiness returns, much to our disappointment. All our journeys to seek pleasure – in this instance, through feeling important – can end in pain and disappointment. Pleasure and pain are two sides of the same coin, as we have discussed, though that is so difficult to see and accept.

How can we approach this fact with intelligence? This need to be important is so hard-wired into our thinking that we never question it. Perhaps we are not even aware of it. Can we just be curious and explore it without regarding it as good or bad or without justifying it? Perhaps we could begin by noticing this need in ourselves and observe the many subtle ways it generates pleasure, shapes our behaviour, and also causes anxiety and stress. The pleasure of being important is always short-lived, whether you become the number one tennis player or the president. Most people are just envious of the famous or important person anyway, no matter what they may say. Or, they want to bask in your reflected glory. Either way, there may be little affection involved. How does being famous affect our relationships?

During my own exploration, I may come upon this ache of emptiness within me from time to time. I need to allow it to be, connecting with it and not escaping from it. How can I learn what it has to teach me if I run away from it each time? As I stay with it and meet the hollow feeling without language, it transforms into a sense of peace. In that peace, that feeling of wanting to be important also seems to fade. I still do what I am doing with passion, but without the drive to be noticed, recognised, and feel important. If that happens as a by-product of my passion, that is fine too, but it is no longer something I chase or judge my life by. With that, so much of my stress seems to melt away. This sense of inner contentment is available to you, and everyone. It is a natural state of mind and being that is accessible to all.

All this may sound simple, but it is not easy. It requires a great deal of exploration. At first, the idea of not being important may feel very strange and you may think it is too far-fetched. Avoid dismissing it out of hand simply because it feels new. It is up to you to explore it for yourself and see what you discover. Do not make it an ideal to pursue either. That does not help. It is an inescapable fact though, that our unconscious need to feel important brings pleasure and shapes our behaviour, but can also be a cause of stress and emotional pain. How can you respond to this fact with your intelligence?

I watch two squirrels in the garden. It is their home. From morning to night, they are just busy with the business of living. Occasionally they will just chase each other up and down the tree, for the sheer fun of it. They seem to not have a care in the world. Their lives seem simple, lived in harmony with the rhythms of nature. I am not sure if they devote any time to being important. Being alive is more than enough.

Explore contentment

Contentment implies peace. Do we live with a sense of peace within?

The human mind has a tendency to take what it already has for granted and to focus on what it does not have. Why is that? We take the people and possessions in our lives for granted, as well as our achievements. Why are we not content, and does that contribute to our stress in any way?

Our discontent pushes us to want things. It fuels our ambition to be successful, to earn more, consume more, and be recognised. If we do not get what we want, we can get stressed.

We could also ask if happiness is contentment. The mind that wants to be happy is dissatisfied and not happy now, but it thinks that it will find happiness in the future. When the future arrives, it remains discontented and chases something else. Could we say that discontentment means happiness always eludes us?

Behind our discontent lies a restless mind that is easily bored and seeks constant stimulation. It is this restlessness that makes us continuously look for something new, overlooking what we already have. Our mind is always asking, "What can I do in the world outside, to make me feel good inside?" No matter what we achieve or how rich we become, this restlessness continues.

This discontent has been important for human achievement, and without it, we may not have achieved all that we have as a human race. We would not have the aeroplane, the submarine, and so on. This discontent has also led to so many wars and deaths, with each country wanting to expand and have more territory. It has also led to overconsumption, with no one being satisfied with what they have, always wanting and consuming more – all of which has contributed to global warming.

At present, this sense of discontent and the unceasing machinations it creates mostly operate unconsciously. How can we respond to it with intelligence? Start by becoming aware of it, without judgement, and see how it operates in our lives. It causes us to take our relationships for granted as well as the things we already have. This awareness may make us appreciate our lives more. We could also ask ourselves, "How much is enough?" A friend of mine recently donated 30 pairs of trousers to charity. Why have so many in the first place?

If we were not discontented, would we lose our energy and drive to do things? Would we just become mediocre? Or, could a passion and love for what we do continue to drive us to excel, but do so with a sense of peace?

NURTURE AND DEEPEN OUR RELATIONSHIPS

Our capacity to cope with stress is diminished if we do not have stable relationships where we can share what we are feeling, feel listened to, cared for, and supported.

The absence of deep and meaningful connections with others can also make us feel lonely, which causes its own stress. This can also occur if we are in a relationship where there is no deep connection or if that relationship is dysfunctional.

Relationships take time to build and require nurturing. When the challenges of life arrive, our relationships need to be in good order to help us meet them. It is too late at that point to start building them or ask for help. People are often unwilling to help others with whom they do not feel a connection.

Studies have shown that close relationships are often the key determinants of our long-term happiness.

What can we do to nurture our relationships, and why do we find it so difficult to have deep and meaningful ones?

Start by realising how important they are in our lives. We take care of and put energy into anything we regard as important – our careers, for example – but we do not lavish the same attention on our relationships. Why is that?

You could begin a journey of self-understanding. Understanding ourselves helps us to understand others better since our minds function in similar ways.

Sometimes the way our mind functions gets in the way of having happy relationships. Here are some examples. We want to be loved, but do not have the same need to love others. We have a need to be listened to, but not to listen. We want to be understood, but do not take the same care to understand. We want others to do things for us, but do not feel the same need to do things for others. We get easily hurt and think that the cause of our pain lies with our friends and not with ourselves (when our expectations are not met, for example). We are critical of others for acting from their self-interest, but do not see that we do the same. Our unconscious need for pleasure pushes us to behave in ways which may hurt others and take advantage of them, and we do not see that. We want power and do not see the harm it can do to our relationships.

The long-term success of our relationships often depends on how we respond when we get hurt.

We have explored how we expect our many emotional needs to be met by others. And if they are not, we feel hurt and may likely feel compelled to blame others for hurting us. We also get hurt when our expectations are not met, when others do not read our signals, or when people say one thing and do another. Again, until and/or unless we work at it, we are usually not aware of the interior mechanics at play in the background. Our first response to feeling hurt is to withdraw our affections, get angry, and move away from people. Many relationships are strained or abandoned because of this one simple fact that was not properly understood or appreciated. We keep the memory of our hurts alive by thinking about them, reliving them over and over. These emotional needs are not wrong, but they do largely operate unconsciously. If we were aware of and are able to examine them, it would present the opportunity for our intelligence to become engaged.

How can we respond to being hurt with intelligence? The first step is to take ownership of that feeling and try not to blame others for how we feel. We could then ask what we can learn about ourselves from that feeling of being hurt. We would see that it is not intelligent to get angry and withdraw our affections because that will just make matters worse. In a relationship, we could share how we are feeling and explore what happened to trigger that feeling in us, but do so in a way that does not blame the other person. This may feel counter-intuitive because the instinct to blame others, move away, and retaliate is so strong. Please give it some consideration because how we respond to feeling hurt will determine the longevity of our relationships. A full discussion about relationships will need to be the subject of another book, but here are some ideas for you to consider:

- You reap what you sow. The more you invest in your relationships, the stronger they become. They need us to give of ourselves, and then give some more, without keeping count. Seize every occasion to nurture them.
- Be aware of your hidden expectations and accept that others are not responsible for meeting them. These expectations are not wrong either. We just need to have a dialogue with each other about them.
- Accept imperfection. Expecting perfection is the beginning of disappointment and conflict. No one is going to be the perfect person we have in our imagination.
- When you get hurt, take responsibility and ask yourself what you can learn about yourself through that. You will always discover something new and that will strengthen your relationship.
- Have the courage to communicate how you are feeling, without blaming the other person for making you feel that way. Do not withdraw or walk away, however tempting that feels.
- Learn to forgive and forget. More on this later.
- Become aware of your self-interest which operates in the background. This awakens intelligence and stops us from taking advantage of others for our own ends.
- If things go wrong, find out what has happened, have the courage to say sorry, and make amends quickly.
- A relationship is dynamic and changes both people, like rivers merging. People change. We change. You are going to have to work at it, regardless of whom you are with. There is no 'perfect person' for you. You just have to find the person you want to travel with.

You may have many friends with whom you communicate on a superficial level and several hundred more on social media. This may make you feel satisfied that you have many friends. These relationships are a good way to stay occupied and can bring us pleasure, but they do not meet our need for a meaningful connection. The number of friends we have is less important than the quality and depth of our relationships, which determines whether they will nourish us and help us navigate the challenges of life.

What can we do to deepen our connection with others?

This needs courage and requires us to be vulnerable and reach out a hand to others without knowing how they will respond. It also needs us to communicate effectively. We need to be able to share our feelings of insecurity and fear with others. We also need to be able to say what we do not like, but in a way that is kind and intelligent. Can we listen to others without judgement, without interrupting or trying to offer advice? Can we understand the meaning behind the words they are using? There is always a risk that the other person will not reciprocate. We cannot expect everyone to like us. We could explore what love is, and this brings with it a realisation that we care primarily about ourselves, which cannot be the basis for a successful relationship. This understanding awakens compassion and a sense of caring for others. We need to stop using others for our own ends and this can happen if we understand our self-interest at work in the background.

All this comes naturally and easily when our inner intelligence is awakened.

Understand our hidden self-interest

Like an iceberg, some of our self-interest is visible to ourselves, but mostly it lies hidden from our awareness. We care about ourselves and all the things we identify with as ours. That is our primary concern. In most situations, our mind is asking, "What can I get out of this?" We are usually unaware of this. Accepting this fact makes us feel uncomfortable because we think that it makes us selfish, and we do not like that label. Or we justify it as just being human, think that nothing is wrong with that, and continue as before. This self-interest impacts our lives in many ways and also contributes to our stress. That is why it needs to be understood, and we cannot do that if we label it as right or wrong.

Our hidden self-interest is one of the main reasons our relationships are challenging and have the potential to generate so much stress. This includes all our relationships: with our children, with ourselves, with family, with work colleagues, with our ideas and beliefs, and with our possessions.

In our relationships, our hidden self-interest is pushing us to get our needs met. This causes conflict because my self-interest is at odds with yours. We can see this in organisations, where people jostle for power, importance, and to go up the ladder. We can also observe this in our homes where we also seek to get others to bend to our will. My needs are paramount and you are important only in as much as you can meet them. If you are not able to meet them, then I get disappointed and lose interest in you, and our relationship ends or gets strained. As a result, we live lonely lives even when we are with people, and this is a significant factor in the stress we feel.

Our self-interest and insecurity also push us to spend our time and energy accumulating wealth. If we are unsuccessful, it can lead to disappointment and stress.

Our self-interest pushes us to search for pleasure through our relationships and our experiences. This can make us use people for our own ends, generating conflict and stress, but we are usually not aware of this.

Our sense of caring is limited to the people we identify with as ours. Since this does not extend to the earth that is our home, we continue to exploit it for our benefit, damaging it in the process. We keep our homes clean and continually try to make them better, but we are trashing our bigger home, the earth. We do not see it, but this is driven by our self-interest to accumulate more wealth and experience.

Our self-interest can also push us to seek out people who look like us, share our language and our opinions and beliefs because this makes us feel comfortable and secure. Being with people who can echo our opinions and beliefs back to us strengthens our sense of self, which always brings pleasure. No one challenges our beliefs because we have created our own echo-chamber. This is how tribes form and one tribe is always in conflict with another tribe. And this is how wars begin, with all their destruction. War affects us all, but we do not see the seeds of that in our thinking.

The self-interest that operates in us also operates in the same way in others. This understanding can awaken compassion. Would we like to be treated in the way we treat others?

Do you find your mind protesting, resisting, and asking, "But how can I live without self-interest?", and then saying to you, "*I do not want to*". This self-interest is at the core of being human, and one of the reasons why we have so many problems. No one is *demanding* that you change. All we are doing is exploring our self-interest in action, without justifying or condemning it. This allows our intelligence to awaken and we will naturally know the right thing to do in each situation. Consider the analogy of driving down a road with many potholes. Activating this intelligence helps us to avoid them.

LET GO OF OUR ATTACHMENT TO OUR VARIOUS IDENTITIES

All of us become unconsciously attached to our various identities and they can become a source of conflict and stress. Why do we human beings get so *attached* to our various identities? Even just contemplating this question could help reduce so much suffering in our world.

I am Indian, Hindu, and speak Hindi. You are Pakistani, Muslim, and speak Urdu.

Or, I am British, Protestant, from Belfast. You are Irish, Catholic, from Dublin.

Or, I am Palestinian, Muslim, speak Arabic, and live in Gaza. You are Israeli, Jewish, speak Hebrew, and live in Israel.

There has been conflict between people attached to these and other identities, for thousands of years. The suffering caused has been unimaginable. Two hundred million people were killed in all the conflicts in the 20th century, many of them between people attached to different identities. Our identities are linked to our nationality, religion, language, and skin colour. We also identify with our possessions, our children, our occupations, our organisations, our opinions, and so on.

How do these identities form? I get unconsciously conditioned by the country, culture, and family I grew up in and adopt those identities without question. I presume this is normal and never question my conditioning influences. I only see the many benefits of having an identity, without seeing the potential dangers which lurk in the shadows, including how such identification can contribute to my stress.

Why do we get attached to our various identities? After all, we may grow up liking chocolate ice cream, or a particular food, but that will never form part of my identity. We would never feel challenged if someone said that our taste in ice cream was terrible or said that vanilla is better. This sounds silly, does it not? The reason we get attached to our countries, religions, and languages is because they meet our hidden emotional needs: a need to belong, to be part of a group, need for pleasure, power, security, and so on. Ice cream does not do that, but our religion and our country do. All this happens unconsciously.

How do these identities cause conflict and stress? If I identify with a particular country or religion and you are critical of that, I can get upset and want to retaliate. If the leader of my country says I need to be a patriot, join the army, and go and kill human beings in another country, I do it without questioning it. Or if my religious leader says that my religion is being attacked and needs defending, I will rally to the cause. If I identify with my football club and if supporters from my club are attacked, I will want to fight because I feel as if I myself have been attacked. I also become attached to people who meet my needs and this can make me jealous: if my wife speaks to another man, for example. I do not see the hidden process of attachment working in the background.

Seeing the stress, anxiety, and sorrow that our attachment to our identities can cause, the intelligent person asks if it is possible to let go of our attachment to all our identities and simply be a human being. This does not mean that I stop going to the temple or church or eating my favourite food, but I do that without an attachment to that particular way of thinking and living in the world. It means I accept that there are other equally valid ways to think and live and that my identity does not divide me from other human beings.

If I am asked to give up my various identities, my first reaction would likely be fear because I am attached to them. Let us say, however, that I am curious, and want to explore this further. I want to find out where my identities came from, why I am attached to them, and the impact this has on my life and the world. I find that it is my *unconscious attachment* to my various identities that causes the problem and not the fact that I may like to visit a temple or church to pray. Can I let go of my *attachment* to my various identities? I also question my unconscious emotional needs, ask where they came from, and ask if I can meet them in other ways. As I kept exploring this subject, to my surprise, I found that these attachments to my various identities disappeared and never came back. I was not the poorer for this in any way, and there was a great sense of freedom. I saw that deep down, all human beings were the same. I became a simple human being and nothing else. I no longer felt attached to any of my old identities and I feel so much richer for it. In the process, so many potential causes of my stress and anxiety also disappeared.

Please explore this for yourself and find out if this understanding also leaves you with this sense of being a simple human being, free of attachment to any identity whatsoever. You may also find that it leaves you feeling free and your life is much richer as a result. I can vouch for that.

This may feel like a radical proposition, especially if like most people, you are attached to your various identities and they bring you pleasure, a sense of belonging, and emotional satisfaction. Why would you even want to consider exploring this?

In response, I would say that no one is *demanding* anything of you. We are just exploring the nature of identity, how it forms, the many ways in which it causes stress, how it contributes to the wars in the world, and also how it also meets our many emotional needs. As you embark on this journey of self-understanding – in this case, exploring the nature of identity – you may discover wisdom, which leads to a sense of peace. In that peace, many of our inner emotional needs change, including our need to be attached to any form of identity. You can be free and contribute to peace in the world. Once the facts are seen clearly, change follows without effort.

UNDERSTAND THE NATURE OF PLEASURE

We have discussed the nature of pleasure earlier in the book, but it is worth exploring further as a means of avoiding stress. The human mind has an overpowering and mostly hidden urge to pursue pleasure in different ways. Using the iceberg analogy again, we can see some of this, but most of this urge operates in the background, directing our actions. This is not wrong, but understanding this allows us to 'avoid the potholes' and live with intelligence.

How can the pursuit of pleasure cause stress? We have explored this earlier, but here are some more examples:

- We use food as a source of pleasure and this can make us obese, with all the psychological and health problems that follow.

- It can push us to drink more alcohol, which is a toxin that can cause cancer and other health problems.
- It can get us addicted to opiates and other drugs. We may begin thinking that we are in control and a bit of pleasure can do no harm, but our urge for pleasure and stimulation is so strong that we lose our self-control, and this results in addiction, which in turn destroys so many lives.
- The more pleasure we seek, the more we seem to need and the less peaceful we feel inside. Our restlessness increases and pushes us to seek more of it, whether it is through shopping, eating, drinking, gambling, or drugs.
- We unconsciously seek to be important because that brings pleasure, and need others to make us feel important. If they do not, we can get frustrated and stressed.
- The search for pleasure awakens desire and makes us pursue many different things in our lives, whether it is fame, wealth, people, possessions, and so on. If we do not get what we want, we can get disappointed and stressed.
- Physical intimacy and affection bring so much pleasure and their pursuit may make us do things that we may later regret, like using people for our own ends or having an affair.

Do you find yourself resisting and saying, "But I do not want to give up my pleasures" or "They are not wrong"? Pleasure is not wrong and in the right context, it is a beautiful feeling at the heart of being human, but understanding it completely and the hidden ways in which it influences our lives, allows us to live with intelligence.

I sat down with some children to explore the nature of pleasure. I was asking the questions and the answers were all theirs. Their responses were most illuminating. This is a snapshot of our conversation.

What do we all want from our lives?

"To be happy."

What are the different things that make you happy?

"Ice cream, holidays, buying things, friends."

How long does the pleasure last?

"Not long. If it is an ice cream, it finishes as soon as it is over, a holiday perhaps a bit longer."

What do you feel when the pleasure ends?

"Bored. Empty. Restless. Lost."

What does the mind want to do next?

"It wants to repeat the pleasure."

But what is different this time?

"It needs to be bigger and better. A bigger toy. A more expensive holiday. More expensive clothes."

What are the implications for our lives?

"It leads to frustration if we cannot get what we want. It can make us spend money we do not have and cause debt."

What are the implications of this for the world?

"It can cause debt, over-consumption, and this contributes to global warming."

So, we have discovered that our need for pleasure is driven by our inner boredom, restlessness, and discontent, which in turn causes over-consumption and this contributes to global warming. How can we solve this problem of our inner boredom? Is it inevitable?

"If you just stay still with your boredom, it goes away."

What is the feeling when your inner boredom goes away?

"I feel peaceful inside."

The children, with their innate wisdom, understood that our need for pleasure comes from a feeling we describe in different ways, but may actually be the same thing. We call it boredom or restlessness or emptiness or a sense of being discontented. All this happens unconsciously. If we can explore and understand the roots of these feelings in ourselves, we can live with intelligence so that our need for pleasure does not act unconsciously and contribute to our distress or result in over-consumption that damages our purse and our planet.

Understand fear

We have explored the nature of fear earlier. We know that many of our fears operate in the background and direct our behaviour. For example, my fear of change may make me justify continuing in an unhappy relationship or job or my fear of illness may make me take unnecessary supplements. How can we prevent the stress caused by fear and anxiety in our lives?

I met a young man who was the head of a college. He was highly educated, very accomplished in many ways, well thought of, and very successful at what he did. He told me that he had suffered from crippling anxiety for many years. He had tried various treatments, all to no avail. These included medication, psychotherapy, and different meditation techniques. He had, however, never explored for himself the nature of fear, and began his own enquiry into it. Many months later, when I met him, he said something had shifted and his anxiety was no longer a problem.

Try this. Get your journal out, write down these questions, and see what emerges in response:

- What are my conscious fears?
- What are my unconscious fears, that operate in the background?
- Is my fear caused by the thing I am anxious about, like my children, or is it linked to an inner process that I am not aware of?
- The next time I am afraid or worried, can I ask, "What can I learn from this about the nature of fear? Is my fear unique to me or is it in every human being?"
- What is the mechanism of fear? Is it caused by my thinking, by my imagination?
- Do I see that imaginary fears have no solution because the problem has not yet occurred?
- How do my fears shape the course of my life?
- How likely is it that the thing that I am afraid of is actually likely to happen? Is it equally likely not to happen?
- Have I been conditioned by something that happened in my past and is that causing my fear?
- Can I accept it and deal with it if it does happen?
- Is there any point in being afraid of something that is inevitable, like losing my looks as I age or dying? Can I accept these as part of life?

- If fear is caused by my thinking, when it arises in me, can I meet it without escaping from it and without thinking? What happens?

Anxiety cannot be ended simply by 'trying not to be anxious'. If the roots of it in our thinking are understood, and this understanding is non-verbal, like a full moon seen clearly, and is not just an idea, it can dissolve. I realise that for many this can seem unachievable and appear like a mountain whose summit is not even visible. In all journeys, the key is to begin. The aim is not to 'solve' the problem of fear, but understand it. One has to understand the entire machinery of thinking because it is one process, even though we study it in its different manifestations. Let go of any goals and just begin travelling inwards, with curiosity, marvelling at the many discoveries you make. On this journey please leave behind all judgement, 'This is right, that is wrong', and just observe and learn. As a natural and effortless by-product of this journey, you will find yourself changed and perhaps wake up one morning and find that fear no longer controls your life, but has its rightful place… and you feel free.

LIVE SIMPLY, WITHIN OUR MEANS

A lack of money generates much of our stress. The Money Advice Service in the UK estimated in 2018 that 8.3 million people in the UK had debt they struggled to service and 22% of the people had less than £100 of savings. Every month since July 2013, the amount borrowed on credit cards has increased. Versions of this are common the world over.

We human beings have created a society with inequality of wealth and income distribution, and this has happened for millennia, with a few exceptions. The poorest people in the developing world live day-to-day, spending what they earn in the day on food for themselves and their families. They only have the clothes they wear and little else. In the richest countries in the world too, people go hungry, and many rely on food banks to get by. In the UK, it is estimated that 500,000 people rely on food banks (Oxfam) and 2% of the population is undernourished (World Bank).

In many parts of the world, cheap credit and advertising push people to spend money they do not have, on things they do not need or on fleeting pleasures. The lack of money does not just cause stress to the poorest in the world. Many people who are in the top 5% of earners in society can also be stressed because their expenditure is more than their income and they live on credit. No matter how much you earn, there is always something you could buy that is just out of reach.

When I was growing up in India, there was no credit available, even to buy homes. My parents lived well within their means and saved for rainy days. The first home they owned was bought with savings. My mother stitched our clothes, we rarely ate out and rarely went away, except to visit family. We never went shopping for fun. We were, however, quite happy, never felt we lacked anything, and just lived simple yet very fulfilled lives. My parents' lifestyle did not change even when their circumstances improved. I was lucky to have been brought up in this environment and had such excellent role models to rely on, and some habits have stuck, like packing a meal to take with me when I am travelling. Others are not so lucky. Whatever our circumstances were while growing up, it is possible to use our intelligence to have a healthy relationship with money and live within our means.

How can we respond, to this problem that the lack of money creates, with intelligence? We may not have enough for our basic needs, life is tough, and there is little room to manoeuvre. Governments have a responsibility to care for the poorest people in society, but what can we as individuals do to manage our money better and not be stressed by the lack of it?

Can we live simpler lives and still be happy? To do this, we need to begin by understanding the hidden nature of conditioning, comparison, and the need for pleasure. They are not wrong, but need to be understood. Without this understanding, any change is much more difficult because these inner forces are powerful and they overcome any obstacle that they encounter, including our willpower.

We do not realise that what we regard as essential in life is influenced by our conditioning. This pushes parents in India, for example, to spend huge amounts of money on weddings or people to think that they need to go on holiday several times a year or change their car every few years. We are also easily conditioned by advertising, which influences our behaviour and may make us buy things that we do not need. We do not have to regard ourselves as 'victims' of this process. Becoming aware of our conditioning and being able to question it allows us to respond appropriately.

We unconsciously compare ourselves with others and want what they have. This also influences our spending habits. We end up borrowing money to spend on things that bring pleasure, but may not be essential for our wellbeing.

Our hidden need for pleasure, which is driven by our inner boredom or emptiness, also influences our spending habits. We have explored how all pleasure is fleeting and the more we have, the more we need. We get pleasure from buying things, going on holiday, eating out, and all this influences our spending habits. If we cannot afford what we want, we can get frustrated and unhappy. If we borrow and spend the money anyway, that creates debt, which generates its own stress. Understanding this could make us explore the inner boredom and restlessness that drives our need for pleasure. This is usually hidden from our awareness. In that exploration, we may find that it transforms into a sense of peace such that our need for pleasure also changes. Pleasure is not wrong, but it usually operates unconsciously, influencing our thoughts and actions.

It is up to each of us to explore how our mind works, ask questions of the life we live, and see if that understanding allows us to live a simpler life. It is not for me to tell you what a simple life looks and feels like – you need to discover the beauty of that for yourself. If we can discover that sense of serenity within ourselves, we may be surprised how little we need to be able to have a deeply fulfilled life.

A simpler life reduces our carbon footprint and is good for the earth. It also helps us live within our means, which reduces the stress that a lack of money can cause. It also allows us to be generous and help others when needed. It comes naturally as part of this inner journey and it does not feel like an effort.

CONNECT WITH NATURE

There is a small wood near my home where I walk regularly. Just a 30-minute stroll is enough to clear my mind and make me feel refreshed, and if I am stressed about something, I feel so much better. Now there is evidence to support the view that being in nature can help reduce stress.

Mary Carol and her colleagues published a paper in *Frontiers in Psychology* in 2019, which showed that 30 minutes of being in nature, three times per week, significantly reduced levels of the stress hormone cortisol in people suffering from stress.

Walking through a wood while chatting with a friend or having a mind that is buzzing with so many thoughts that we hardly notice the birds does not bring the same benefits. It is more important to feel a sense of *connection* with nature.

I like this poem from the Chinese poet Li Po, which conveys this well: "All the birds have flown up and gone; a lonely cloud floats leisurely by. We never tire of looking at each other – Only the mountain and I".

There is a tall poplar tree near my home. It is a source of endless delight. When the sun catches its leaves and there is a slight wind, it seems every leaf is dancing with joy at being alive. Looking at it in all its splendour is mesmerising and it makes me forget myself. I feel a deep sense of connection to it, and in the process, I discover that whatever stress I was carrying with me just goes away.

Being in nature grounds us to the present. Otherwise, we can live in our imagination, in the thoughts buzzing in our minds. Having this ability to connect with nature needs to be part of our education and is far more important than learning facts that we soon forget, however important we may think them to be.

Connecting non-verbally with nature is important because we can apply the same process to explore our inner spaces. When we look at a flower, our tendency is to name it or say, "How beautiful!", and carry on walking or chatting with a friend. Try this instead. Pause a while. Look at it without a single thought coming between you and the flower. Notice its texture, the play of light and shadow on it, and allow its beauty to seep in without calling it beautiful. We discover so much more about a flower when we look at it this way. Now stay with it for a while, like Li Po, the poet. Notice how your mind becomes still and there is that vast sense of calm and peace within. Can you look at your thoughts and feelings in a similar way, non-verbally, just observing them without language?

Why is connecting with nature so beneficial? That is a mystery. Perhaps it is because we are a part of it, made up of the same basic building blocks of matter as the river and the universe.

If we felt this sense of connection with nature, it could help us avoid stress.

THE ROLE OF EXERCISE

The mind and body are one unitary organism. Stress affects our physical health and results in changes at a cellular level in our body. If we do not look after our physical health, it can affect us mentally too. Exercise is a simple way of helping us boost our mental health and prevent many diseases.

Regular aerobic exercise has been shown to be good for our mental health in a number of studies. It improves mood, vitality, sleep, and also helps treat mild depression and anxiety disorders. The benefits are also seen in diabetes, heart disease, chronic pain, and some cancers. It may play a role in the prevention of dementia. The Chief Medical Officers in the UK published activity guidelines in 2019. For adults, they recommend 150 minutes of moderate activity a week (brisk walking, swimming, or cycling), or 75 minutes of vigorous activity a week (running, sport, or climbing stairs). With moderate activity, you should still be able to have a conversation, but with vigorous activity, you should not. This should be combined with two days of muscle-strengthening a week (yoga, weights).

There are two groups of theories to explain why exercise helps reduce stress – psychological and physiological.

Exercise can distract us from unhappy thoughts. The confidence in our ability to achieve a challenging task like exercise can boost our confidence and mood in other areas of our life.

Exercise results in the release of beta-endorphin, which is an opioid. It acts on our central nervous system to make us feel calm and boost our mood. Research also shows that regular exercise reduces cellular inflammation, creates more neurotransmitters in our brain, and releases trophic factors, all of which have many benefits. Recent research suggests that it may also improve the mix of bacteria we have in our gut microbiome, and this has many benefits as well.

For all the evidence of the benefits of exercise, it is surprising how few people actually do any. The US Department of Health estimates that 28% of the population does not do any exercise at all, and only one in three adults does the recommended amount of exercise a week. The numbers are likely to be similar or worse elsewhere. Why is that? What is it in our thinking that somehow stops us from doing the things that we *know* are essential for a healthy life? One reason could be that we always have so many things to do 'right now' that feel like a priority, and though exercise is important, it does not seem as pressing. The less one exercises, the less one feels like exercising, and our inertia grows. Or, we may live in an environment where nobody exercises and we become conditioned to follow that. Whatever the reason, and there will be many more, self-understanding allows us to do the right thing and get past the obstacles in our thinking that stop us from looking after our health.

Get enough sleep

Stress can affect our sleep, keeping us awake at night, but poor sleep can in turn increase our stress, irritability, and inability to cope, and is linked to many health problems. It can become a vicious cycle.

The American Sleep Association recommends between seven to nine hours of sleep for adults per night. Its surveys show that 35% of Americans get less than seven hours of sleep a night. In the UK, the Sleep Council estimates that one in three adults gets less than six hours of sleep a night.

Research suggests that inadequate sleep can increase our risk of getting diabetes, obesity, heart disease, depression, anxiety, and weaken our immune system, making us more prone to getting the flu, for example. It can also shorten our lifespan. Poor sleep can affect short- and long-term memory, our ability to concentrate, and our sex drive.

It is, therefore, vital that we prioritise it and get it right.

Regular exercise can help us sleep better, as can having a fixed bed-time, avoiding screen time before bed, avoiding caffeine after lunchtime, and reading or meditating before bed. Reducing the stress in our lives can help us sleep better too.

Why are some of us unable to get enough sleep which we know is essential for a healthy life? Is it because we are stressed and the activities of the day keep churning away in our thinking, keeping us awake? Or do we feel we have so much to do that cutting back on sleep is the only way to get all the jobs done? Or perhaps we have developed such a strong need for stimulation and pleasure that we stay up watching one screen or another into the night? Whatever the reason and there will be others, understanding ourselves and the way our minds work allows us to get past these obstacles that stop us from leading healthy lives.

GET YOUR DIET RIGHT

Stress results in excessive levels of the hormone cortisol in our blood, which can increase our appetite and make us crave for food with a high fat and sugar content. We have explored how food and the pleasure it brings, provides a psychological distraction from our stress. This process happens unconsciously and results in obesity with its many health problems which can cause stress in turn. If we are obese, then we may have to deal with body image issues, which can exacerbate our stress.

There are claims that certain foods may help us avoid stress, but in doing my research, I was not convinced, and you will have to make your own mind up.

There are, however, well-researched health benefits of having a well-balanced plant-dominant diet, eating in moderation, keeping our weight in check, and staying well hydrated.

Exercise, adequate sleep, and a good diet contribute to our physical health, which in turn supports our mental health. Why do so many of us find it so difficult to follow this advice? The answer unsurprisingly lies in our thinking, in understanding how our mind works.

DOES IT MATTER?

If you find yourself getting stressed, a simple question may help end it before the stress gains momentum: does it matter? In all our relationships, people have a certain way of doing things that are different from our own. If we do not ask this question, then we can get stressed by innumerable little things that happen through the day: the way they leave their clothes on the floor, or unwashed dishes near the sink, or leave the cap off the toothpaste, and so on.

Try this. Write down a list of all the day-to-day things that cause stress, and then ask yourself for each of them, "Does it matter?" You may find that other people just have different preferences, and if you look at the big picture, perhaps it does not matter at all. All it needs is for us to change our perspective and look at things from other people's point of view. If you can do this, then all the minor daily stresses of your life can end.

If you can deal with small stresses in this way, then the same process applies to bigger ones: the annoying habits that people close to you have, the fact that you have a small car and a small house compared to others, and so on.

Changing our perspective and realising that most things do not *really* matter can help us avoid much of the stress we experience. If it *does* matter, then you can have a relaxed conversation about it and sort it out devoid of any irritation and frustration in your voice.

LIVING WITH AWARENESS

A thrush sings in the garden as I write this. It is a glorious spring day, but there is a chill in the air. I am aware of all this, but also notice that I am thinking about a conversation I had with my sister earlier. I am not fully present and my thoughts wander off from time to time.

Living with awareness is not easy, but is at the centre of this approach to meeting life and its challenges in a completely fresh way. This awareness takes in what is happening in the world around us and what is happening in the world within, in a seamless manner. It is this awareness which allows us to notice envy arising in ourselves and the process of comparison behind it, or the irritation that we may feel from seeing unwashed dishes near the sink, or our urge to interrupt a friend in a conversation and share that 'Oh so relevant!' opinion… and accept that it does not matter.

How can we carry this awareness with us throughout the day? It comes through a seamless synthesis of learning the art of looking at ourselves, a meditative mind that is sensitive to the world and open to learning about itself, and an understanding of the many hidden patterns of thinking that operate behind the scenes. It is a life-long journey of learning, and as the art of asking and enquiring become suffused into your daily activities, life can be so much richer for it.

In the next chapter, we are going to explore the role of meditation in avoiding and managing stress.

THE ROLE OF MEDITATION
AND STILLNESS

THERE IS PLENTY OF EVIDENCE that meditation can help us manage stress. It can, however, be confusing because the same word is used by people to describe many different ideas and practices. It is essential to explore the question of meditation in depth, from different perspectives, so if we are interested, we set about it in a perceptive way.

WHAT IS MEDITATION?

Meditation has been practised in many different cultures for millennia. *The Oxford Dictionary* defines meditation as a "practice of thinking deeply in silence, especially for religious reasons or in order to make your mind calm". Other definitions include: "to engage in contemplation or reflection" and "to think calm thoughts in order to relax or as part of a religious activity". The word 'meditation' is also used to describe a technique involving focused attention on an object, or one's breathing, or teaching calmness or compassion. In popular culture, many think it is a technique to quieten the mind. It is much more important to go beyond the word 'meditation' and explore what it points to. The word 'moon', for example, does not communicate the experience of looking at it for yourself. Perhaps exploring a series of questions related to meditation may help us understand it better. And then, ultimately, you will need to practice it for yourself.

WHAT IS WISDOM?

Why is wisdom important, and what does it have to do with stress? We make so many mistakes in our lives and looking back, we wish we had

had a deeper understanding that could have helped us avoid them. So much of our stress is generated by our own thinking and actions and a deeper understanding of that process could have helped us avoid so much of it. Perhaps this understanding is wisdom.

Does wisdom come with experience, as popular thinking suggests? As you get older, gathering a lot of experience, does that automatically make you wise?

In the world outside, knowledge accumulated over many years does give you a deeper understanding of your particular subject. Some people would call that wisdom. If you have been a farmer for 40 years, you will have an intuitive understanding of the land and crops, which a younger person may not have. I remember seeing a patient with back pain, that he said he had had for a few months. A younger me would have just ordered a scan of his back, seen it was okay, and sent him away. I do not know what it was about him that made me suspect something else was going on. You could call it intuition. I ordered a scan of his abdomen, even though he had presented with back pain. The scan showed he had cancer of the pancreas and he had surgery for it straight away.

When it comes to life in general and our inner spaces, do our accumulated experiences bring wisdom? Is a person who is 80 years old wiser than a child of eight? Perhaps. Wisdom may not have anything to do with age. You may carry all your prejudices with you as you age and repeat them to everyone, or you may generalise from your experiences and say, for example, that people of a certain community or country are not to be trusted. All our conditioning influences become the foundation for our opinions, beliefs, and behaviour, and since all our conditioning is so limited, so is our opinion. We are certain that we are right and the older we are, the more certain we become. We also believe others should listen to us because we know and they do not, which creates conflict.

Does wisdom come from books, considering that they may be written by the wisest people and be centuries old? You may read a dozen books telling you what the moon looks like and be able to repeat them, but you will only experience its beauty by seeing it for yourself.

Again, I suggest that wisdom comes from a deeper understanding of ourselves and how our mind works, which awakens inner intelligence. The wise person knows that he or she does not know everything, and is not attached to his or her narratives. The other benefits of wisdom include having happy relationships because you understand others better, meeting life's challenges with serenity, and living with compassion and a sense of peace. Each of us need to discover this wisdom for ourselves.

WHY DO WE WANT TO MEDITATE?

Most of us begin because we want it to help us in some way. We may be stressed or anxious or feel a lack of peace within and believe that meditation will help us be healthier and calmer. Others think that meditation offers an understanding of spirituality and they want to be 'enlightened', whatever that word may mean to them. Some may see others doing it and want to join in. Increasingly, people are drawn to meditation to help them fulfil their career goals or enhance their performance in business or athletics. Even the army has taken this up as a way of helping soldiers deal with stress.

No matter what the genesis, rarely do we want to begin to meditate if we are already happy, when pleasure exists in abundance in our lives.

Let us say a person is distressed, wants to not be so, and has concluded that meditation is the answer. We rarely ask ourselves *why* we are distressed or unhappy in the first place nor do we explore the origins of that in our thinking. Without that understanding, the underlying patterns of thinking that generate my unhappiness, stress, and anxiety will continue to operate. We mostly tell ourselves: *I hope that meditation will help reduce my stress and anxiety in some way and make me feel better.* There is nothing wrong with that and meditation will probably help, but it may not bring freedom from the underlying patterns of thinking that generated the stress in the first place. It is similar to taking paracetamol for fever and not exploring and treating the actual cause of it. The temperature will come down, but the underlying cause of the fever will continue. Meditation, in this context, may help reduce the symptoms of stress that a person feels, but may not stop those feelings from recurring. Perhaps the practice of meditation needs to be combined with a deeper understanding of the patterns of thinking that contribute to our distress in the first place.

WHY IS IT DIFFICULT TO FIND THE MOTIVATION TO MEDITATE REGULARLY?

We all want to live as long as possible and be healthy till the last moment, and yet we find it difficult to follow the evidence that tells us how to do so. We have explored the benefits of getting enough sleep, exercising 150 minutes/week, eating the right food, and doing regular meditation. Despite knowing this, why do we find it so difficult to motivate ourselves to do so? On the other hand, we do not need much motivation to drink or eat in excess. We human beings are a collection of paradoxes, not able to use our intelligence to look after ourselves, even though we know what we need to do. Why is that?

Perhaps it is because of the force of our hidden needs. They can have the power to obscure the ability of our 'intelligent mind' to discern what is good for us. These needs are powerful and can seize our full attention – driving our activities and leaving little room for 'sensible stuff' that we know is good for us. There is the need for pleasure, for example, which may come from eating and drinking, and this need overpowers any thought which stands in its way. We know this is unhealthy but cannot seem to stop ourselves. We are busy earning a livelihood and our inner insecurity makes us want to accumulate more and more. We also want to have 'fun,' and there seems to be 'no time' for regular exercise or meditation. Like all good intentions that get postponed until tomorrow, they never find their way into the routine of our lives. I exaggerate deliberately to make a point. There are, of course, many people who live healthy lives and balance the need to make a living with the need to look after the mind and body.

Some people find it difficult to meditate and get frustrated that they are unable to quieten their mind. Why is that?

When we first sit down to meditate, the mind is usually busy with thoughts, remembering different things that have happened during the day. Meditators then use whatever technique they practice to try and still the mind. Many may find this difficult at first and their thoughts keep buzzing away. Some may even conclude, "I find it difficult to meditate" or "I am no good at meditating". Or, they switch tactics and try focusing their thinking on something else, like an object, or do some chanting, and hope that it will have a better effect.

What is going on?

The reason that 'I' find it difficult to meditate may be because the 'I' that wants to meditate is created by thinking, though that is not immediately apparent. So, the same 'I' is trying to silence one thought with another thought, and that is fundamentally not possible. The meditator may also have a predetermined idea of what meditation should be, which is a quiet mind, and if this is not 'achieved', the conclusion is that 'I have failed'. Perhaps there is no goal to achieve and the very 'having' of a goal is what is impeding, rather than helping, our practice.

DOES MEDITATION HAVE A GOAL?

How does having a goal influence my meditation practice?

Having a goal implies having an idea of what the endpoint will be. Most of us who meditate have a goal in mind, something we want to get out of it for ourselves. We may not be aware of this. It could be to feel calm, or to have compassion, or be enlightened, or to have a beautiful experience, or experience silence, or be less stressed or anxious. Our mind is used to establishing goals and going after them.

Having a goal implies measurement. I measure how I am now and then how I am when I finish my meditation. It implies comparison because I compare how I am before and after my meditation practice. I may also compare myself with others and how well they are doing.

If I achieve my goal, I will be happy and keep going. If I do not achieve my goal, I can get frustrated and blame the meditation practice or myself. I may also experience the anxiety of comparing myself with others or feel like a 'failure' if I cannot meditate.

Is it possible to meditate without having a goal in mind? That leaves you open to discovering the unknown and the unimagined and be completely surprised when you do come across an insight or the beauty of deep silence. You can also avoid the frustration of not reaching a predetermined 'goal' and giving up as a result.

WHAT ARE THE DIFFERENT TYPES OF MEDITATION PRACTICE?

There are different practices of meditation that have evolved over time. Each of them has its advocates. There are two basic types of meditation practice: one is focused on a phrase or breath or object or image and the other type is an open awareness of what is happening in the present. Both involve sitting in a quiet space once or twice a day for fixed periods of time.

Vipassana, which has its origins in Buddhism, focuses on insight and what is happening in the present moment, without judgement. It has been made secular and popularised as Mindfulness.

Zen meditation, which dates back to the seventh century, involves following one's breath. It may also involve focusing on a puzzle or 'koan'.

Metta or Loving-kindness meditation involves directing loving thoughts towards oneself and then to others. It has its origins in Buddhism and Hinduism.

Transcendental Meditation, or TM, is a silent form of mantra meditation where a specific phrase is recited repeatedly.

Body-scan meditation, or progressive relaxation, is a technique that encourages people to scan their bodies for areas of tension and release them.

Chanting meditation involves chanting a prayer or some other phrase and is part of the spiritual practice of many religious traditions.

Yoga and t'ai chi are movement-based practices that could be considered meditative if done with a deep awareness of the mind and body.

More recently, 'guided meditations' have become popular, with someone speaking to you while you meditate. Many people find this helpful, hence its popularity. If meditation is about exploring silence, I wonder how someone talking to us at the same time can help us do that.

In my view, all these practices can be helpful, but have their limitations, as I will explore later.

THE MEDITATIVE MIND

Many of our images of meditation are of people sitting cross-legged somewhere quiet with their eyes closed. Is that essential or can we also meditate with our eyes open, sitting in a garden? Do I need to close my eyes to observe my thoughts? Can we also observe them with our eyes open? Observing does not require thinking. We can look at a flowing stream without naming it, just observing its every detail. If we become aware of the automatic process of thinking, which names everything we see, it stops and our mind quietens down. In that quietness, we can also observe the random thoughts that come and go in our mind, without naming them, engaging with them, or judging them. We can watch them as we watch that stream, or a bird flying across the sky, or a cloud floating by.

This is the meditative mind and it is alive throughout the day, not just when we sit down to meditate with our eyes closed. It is sensitive to the beauty of the world, to people, and to the many patterns of thinking that operate behind the screen of our awareness. When fear arises in us, for example, the meditative mind is awake and can observe that and learn something new. This awareness of what is happening in the world around us and in our thinking allows us to respond to life with intelligence. A welcome by-product of this intelligence is that there seems to be much less stress in our life.

WHAT ARE THE BENEFITS OF MEDITATION?

There are many research papers that attest to the benefits of meditation, with most focusing on Mindfulness Meditation. It has been shown to have a beneficial effect in the following ways:

- Reduction in stress
- Reduction in anxiety
- Beneficial impact on depression
- Reduction in pain in chronic pain sufferers
- Positive impact in treating addiction
- Beneficial in eating disorders
- Improvement in attention span
- Improvement in memory
- Boost in our immune system

Several imaging studies have shown that meditation can result in a change in brain structure with an increase in the thickness of the pre-frontal cortex, and early research suggests this may slow the cognitive decline associated with aging.

From the perspective of this book and an enquiry into how our mind works, meditation complements this approach. A quiet mind is less reactive, allowing intelligence the space to act.

Given these benefits, perhaps we all need to include a meditation practice in our daily lives, alongside eating the right food in moderation, regular exercise, and getting enough sleep.

THE LIMITATIONS OF MEDITATION

Having just listed all the benefits of meditation, it may seem strange to explore its limitations. It is important to reflect on them, however, so that our practice may avoid these limitations and go beyond them.

This is not meant as a criticism of individuals or their meditation practice, but I know people who have meditated regularly for many years, yet when the challenges of life arrive, they revert back to old patterns of thinking and behaviour. Why is that?

Perhaps meditation provides little insight into the hidden patterns of thinking that cause our stress. It allows us to observe our thoughts and perhaps find some calm, but does not contribute to the penetrative enquiry that can end stress at its root. As a result, these patterns of thinking that generate our stress and sorrow continue to rock our lives. For example, most of the stress and anxiety caused by social media is because our mind unconsciously compares itself with others regularly. This is essential for life in many ways but can also result in envy. To get rid of the stress that our envy generates, we may meditate and it will help us be calmer, but the next day when we go on social media again, the same process is triggered and our anxiety comes back. If, on the other hand, we have a deep insight and awareness into the nature of comparison and realise that the way in which it affects our life is just not intelligent, it can melt away. When we then go on to social media, we experience no anxiety because we no longer compare ourselves with others.

We may have many emotional needs that we are not aware of and we can also look to meditation to meet those needs, without being aware that we are doing so. Joining a meditation class may make us feel less alone, for example.

When people become attached to a particular belief system (which may advocate a specific practice of meditation), they can feel challenged when confronted by people who adhere to a different belief system. This can result in violence, and examples of this are apparent in different parts of the world. The paradox is that all the people involved in the conflict follow belief systems that advocate love and peace. But, since the roots of identity and conflict in our thinking are not understood, violence ensues and we end up justifying it to ourselves as being triggered by others. Meditation does not seem to be able to stop this.

Meditation can also become about 'me': my needs, my peace, my enlightenment, and my well-being. Any preoccupation with the 'me' strengthens the sense of self, and though it is not apparent, the 'self' or the 'I' is behind much of our psychological distress. There is thus a paradox there that is not easy to resolve. Perhaps in exploring the way our mind works, alongside our meditation practice, we can find a happy balance.

THE IMPORTANCE OF UNDERSTANDING THE 'I' WHO MEDITATES

In a previous chapter, we have explored the question of 'Who suffers?'. A similar question is 'Who meditates?'. Understanding the meditator has to be at the heart of any meditation practice.

It is not easy to comprehend that our mental suffering is caused by the structure of the 'I'. It is the 'I' that experiences stress, anxiety, and suffering. The same thinking process that creates the 'I' also experiences the suffering and then hopes to end it through meditation. Meditation becomes a fire extinguisher to put out the fire of stress. Understanding the nature of the 'I' is like discovering the root cause of the fire, so that it does not ignite in the first place, doing away with the need for a fire extinguisher.

Meditation and this understanding complement each other and can go hand-in-hand. Meditation on its own is limited, but it still has many proven benefits. Understanding the nature of the self and our fears, pleasures, and sorrows needs a curious and sensitive mind, able to notice and explore its inner spaces. This is made easier through meditation that makes our mind more open, sensitive, and quiet. A quiet mind is less reactive, allowing space for intelligence to operate.

We have explored how our reactions are a way to learn about ourselves and how our mind works, and through that exploration, a way to observe the nature of the 'I' and how it is put together by our thinking. This loosens our attachment to our opinions, beliefs, and all the things we identify with as ours. As a result, many of the causes of our stress can just dissolve.

Because our reactions reveal our conditioning and the nature of our thought processes like fear, it follows that we need to be able to observe them as they arise in us, and this can occur throughout the day. If I am meditating for only 30 minutes a day, I am going to miss all the learning opportunities that the rest of the day brings. This is why it is important to carry our 'living awareness' with us as we go through the day.

When I am sitting still and observing my thoughts, I notice that there is a loss of attention, and my thoughts wander off. I am not aware of the moment when they do that. I then 'wake up' to the fact that I have been daydreaming and come back to the present. I can remember what I have just been thinking. I then become aware of my breathing and the world around me until the cycle repeats itself.

Why does this happen? Why can 'I' not control my thinking and stop my thoughts from wandering off? What does that reveal about the nature of the 'I'? Perhaps this suggests that the 'I' that is recording and observing everything is just another thought. The implications of this for our meditation practice are profound.

A meditation practice implies that there is the 'I' implementing that method, whether it is reciting a mantra or practising mindfulness. Therefore, with these practices, we are unlikely to connect with that deep nourishing silence because thought, in the form of the 'I', is still operating. Any meditation practice that ignores an enquiry into the 'I' will not touch that silence. You are right to say, "But then, what am I to do?" Can you observe how our mind always seeks a method and wants to be told what to do? Can we begin our own journey of enquiry, ask the questions freshly of ourselves, and see what we discover? In that enquiry, one may stumble upon that elusive silence, as we will explore later.

It is a paradox that the 'I' that begins this journey of enquiry and practice of meditation is itself a barrier to discovering the truth of the nourishing silence it seeks. Connecting with that silence is like drinking from the fountain ourselves, rather than reading about how wonderful the water tastes. The only way we can resolve this paradox is firstly to be aware of it, and then, to include an exploration of the 'I' as we travel. Understanding the meditator needs to be at the heart of our enquiry and our practice of meditation.

This enquiry into the nature and structure of the 'I', alongside a more formal meditative practice, leaves me with a feeling of peace. This peace is a by-product of this enquiry and is not something that was a goal when I started exploring my inner spaces.

THE FOUR DIMENSIONS OF AWARENESS

When I sit down to meditate and start being aware of what is going on, there are four dimensions that my awareness covers.

The first is the world around me, the sounds and smells of my environment. Today this included the sound of a distant plane, the wind rushing through the trees, and the smell of bread baking in the kitchen.

The second is my body and the sensations coming from it. My joints may be hurting from sitting cross-legged, for example, or I may be hungry, tired, or have a headache. I may be aware of my breathing and the rise and fall of my chest.

The third dimension of awareness is my thoughts and feelings. They are pretty random and I observe them as they come and go. I cannot stop them. I find that I am usually aware of them after they have occurred.

The fourth dimension of awareness, and one which is often overlooked, is the 'I' observing and recording all the other three dimensions. This is the most crucial observation and yet the most challenging. What clues can I offer you as you begin to explore it? I can offer no method. As you sit, just be aware of the 'I' recording everything. As you become aware of it, the silence deepens, and you are left just with the sensation of breathing. You have to drink the water to find out what it tastes like. No description or method can take you there.

Can awareness during our meditation practice include all the four elements, without judgement, just observing them?

A SIMPLE BREATHING EXERCISE

This is a simple breathing exercise I use throughout the day and as part of a formal meditation practice.

I focus on my breath entering and leaving my nose. As I breathe in, I notice the air is slightly cooler and as I breathe out, it is slightly warmer. The difference is subtle.

I do this several times a day, whenever there is a spare moment. It snaps me out of my ruminative thinking process that becomes disconnected from the reality of life in the moment. It connects me to my surroundings and my awareness kicks in, allowing space for intelligence to act. It also calms me down, allowing me to reflect on what is happening in the world around me and in my thinking. I become aware that my thoughts are a product of my conditioning and are not real. All this happens effortlessly.

THE BEAUTY OF SILENCE, BEYOND THINKING

I was sitting in a café talking to a friend when the silence descended upon me like a warm embrace. We were exploring the way our minds work and gradually, imperceptibly, it was there. That silence was felt by the mind and the body and there was no divide between the two. I found that my mind had become extraordinarily quiet and was able to see very clearly, with a heightened sense of awareness. In that silence, I was able to notice everything, all at once, instead of one at a time. There was the sound of people talking in the next room, of the coffee machine, of the birds singing outside, and of cups being put away. I noticed the details of the decor: the placemats, the pictures on the walls, and the staff behind the counter. I felt connected to everyone and everything there, and it was quite beautiful. It did not feel like an 'experience', and there was no pleasure or a feeling that it was happening *to* me. There was no sense of the 'me' present recording it all. I did not deliberately try and notice my breathing, as I would in a meditative practice, but there was a heightened awareness of it. I noticed that my mind had ceased to be reactive and I was able to listen to my friend with deep silence and pause for a long time before responding. I was able to continue having a conversation, but there was a depth and clarity to it that felt fresh. There was an awareness of an inner sound, in the background, which was continuous, but it did not interfere with the silence. My usual sense of restlessness was missing. There was a deep sense of peace, of not wanting anything more from life than being in that moment. It was enough.

Words cannot do that silence justice. It perhaps lasted 30 minutes but felt much longer than that. Just as quietly as it had arrived, it left, and there was no resistance to its leaving. It had come unexpectedly and left of its own accord. I did not make anything more of it or draw any inferences from it. The silence felt different from the silence you feel when you are in a quiet room, or the silence between thoughts, or when the music stops. This silence was otherworldly, achingly beautiful, and without reason.

I say this tentatively because I am not sure, but perhaps this silence lies beyond thinking when the sense of 'me' is absent, and the normal chatter of the mind ceases. I felt I just came upon it, as part of this journey of enquiry, and not because I was looking for it. All you need to do is to set out on this journey of learning about yourself.

May you come upon it too.

HOW CAN WE RESPOND TO STRESS WITH INTELLIGENCE?

WE HUMAN BEINGS ARE SO capable when it comes to solving the problems that we encounter in the world around us, but struggle to resolve the problems that emerge from our inner spaces, and stress is foremost among them. How can we apply our intelligence to solve this problem? Our intelligence can respond, now that we have a much deeper understanding of the roots of our stress in our thinking, how our mind works, the nature of stress, and how our mind normally responds to stress.

As we have previously explored, both meditation and exercise help us to avoid stress and deal with it when it does arise, but there are several other things we can do as well. **Pause. Breathe. Slow the stress reaction down.**

We know that the human mind is reactive, and when it reacts, it can cause stress. We have explored that the reactive mind is not intelligent. This is because we react to any situation from a small bit of our conditioning, and can usually not contemplate any other way to see things or a different way to respond. Our reactions can be powerful and tend to repeat themselves. This is the nature of conditioning. How can we use this understanding to respond with intelligence?

The first step is to recognise that we are in the middle of a stress reaction and then observe this unconscious reactivity without judging it as good or bad. This is not easy at first, as we are so emotionally charged and upset. In the midst of this reaction, when the fire is burning in our mind, there are a hundred thoughts and feelings coming at us simultaneously, and we struggle to make sense of them or know what to do. We blame others, try to distract ourselves in some way, and lose perspective. We try to 'think' our way out of our stress, but we find that it does not help and can add to the fire. It is like trying to put out the fire with the same fuel that started it. If you can have an awareness that your mind is reacting and that is causing stress, you can then see that any action based on that reaction is unlikely to be intelligent. So, you pause. Take a breath and slow things down.

Our thinking is often unable to solve the problem of stress because our stress reaction comes from our thinking. Test it for yourself and see. What *can* make a difference is the understanding of the hidden patterns of thinking that cause our stress in the first place. For this understanding to act, we need space in our thinking and a clear mind.

What can we do to slow our reaction down? We can begin by noticing small reactions. For example, when you are listening to someone and you observe yourself reacting with an urge to say something, just pause there and watch that reaction. Or, if the conversation is not interesting, observe how your mind wanders away. Watch that and keep listening. In the beginning, the awareness is usually after the reaction has occurred. We have explored the three stages of insight, and we need to get to the second stage where we notice the reaction as it is occurring. This takes awareness and energy.

If you can notice small reactions and respond with awareness and non-judgement, then you can notice the big reactions in the same way.

Breathing exercises, like the one I described earlier, can help. Tuning into your breathing grounds you to the present. As you feel a reaction coming, just pause, tune into your breathing, and watch the stress reaction inside you as it arises. Meet it gently, without resistance, allowing it to wash over you like a wave on a seashore. Just stay with it and resist the temptation to escape. It rises, peaks, and then fades if it is not sustained by the oxygen of more thinking.

This ability to pause, breathe, and take a step back is a crucial first step to opening the door to allow our intelligence to operate. It is similar to a first aid response where we react instinctively to a challenge because we have practised the drill before.

There were many times in my career where this was very useful in responding to challenging and stressful situations like complaints from patients, complications during surgery, or dealing with difficult colleagues. Once the initial acute stress reaction passes, we can have clarity and can then respond with intelligence.

You too can apply this practice to your life. Begin today, noticing the next stress reaction you have. This is not easy, but once you know what is happening, it is much easier to spot.

Okay, you have got to the first step of noticing that you are getting stressed. What next? Understand that it is a reaction from your conditioning and stopping it is not easy. So, before you react to it, just pause, breathe in, and breathe out ever so slowly, counting to ten (if you can) as you do so. Now you have some space to look at what is happening and respond with intelligence.

ZOOM OUT

We have explored how stress makes us focus on a perceived threat or – to borrow a popular term from modern software – 'zoom' into it. This served our ancestors well by bringing all our attention to the problem so we may activate the flight or fight response, and was essential for our survival. Sometimes 'zooming in' is very helpful, when faced with a physical threat, for example, but more often than not, we need to do the opposite. In modern life, it does not serve us as well, and may in fact make us lose our perspective and narrows our ability to respond appropriately.

Here it is perhaps useful to pause and explore the difference between physical threats, like a poisonous snake, for example, and psychological threats to the 'I', for instance, when we are criticised. Our mind does not differentiate between the two and thinks that they are the same. That is why when we are criticised, or our opinion is challenged, or we are not made to feel important, we respond in the same way as if we are being physically attacked. It is vital that we use our intelligence to understand this difference because the response to the two threats perhaps needs to be completely different. I would suggest that psychological challenges are better dealt with not by 'zooming in' and reacting to them, but by 'zooming out' and allowing our intelligence the space to respond.

The intelligent response in most stressful situations we face is to zoom out and maintain that more global perspective. It allows us to see that no problem, however significant it may feel, is the end of the world. We all could avoid so much anguish if we followed this simple practice in response to stress. It may be simple, but that does not mean that it comes easily to everyone. It can require considerable repetition, discipline, and restraint, however, it is a tool available to all.

In practice, 'zooming out' means seeing the problem in the context of a month or a year or five years. It could mean looking at yourself from the moon, for example, and realising how insignificant we and our problems truly are. Or, knowing that in the context of a whole life this particular problem is nothing (like the end of a marriage), and it is all part of the rich tapestry of the human experience.

How can we do that during a stressful crisis? It is a challenge. That is why we first need to practice with lesser crises and minor, everyday disturbances. Does it matter how someone stacks the dishwasher, or how they hang the clothes out to dry, or if you have a flat tyre, or a flight gets cancelled? If we can manage to *zoom out* in small stressful situations, then when the big challenges come, like the loss of a job or ill health, we are ready and find it easier to do so.

When a relationship ends, it can generate so much conflict, anger, and sorrow. Each person thinks that they have been wronged in some way and justify their anger, which can sometimes continue for years. If both people had this ability to zoom out, they would realise that in the context of an entire life, it does not matter as much as we think it does. Each person will go on to have other relationships and build a life again. The children will probably continue to love both parents dearly and grow up to be well-rounded people.

Zooming out may also stop us from doing things that we may later regret: hurting ourselves or others, buying something we cannot afford, or taking an extra dose of drugs or alcohol.

You have likely heard these kinds of stories – there are so many of them if you choose to look: people who are initially distraught at losing their jobs, for example, but eventually go on to build other careers. Or, people whose businesses fail and who may think it is a disaster, but go on to be successful at something else entirely. Or, young people who struggle to pass exams or finish college, but go on to have good careers. Zooming out has many advantages, but it is not something our mind does instinctively. In reality, it does the opposite. Seeing this fact allows us to respond with intelligence.

Be grateful

We have explored how our mind often takes what we already have for granted, and instead yearns for what we do not have, either materially or emotionally. That is just the way our human mind functions. You can see this in homes where many objects gather dust: shoes, electronics, handbags, decorative objects, and so on. They once brought great pleasure, but now we barely notice them. We also take our homes and the people in our life for granted. We always want something more or different.

Why is our mind like that?

Perhaps it is because it is looking to be stimulated, to move away from the moment it is in, usually through pleasure because it offers a distraction from the inner boredom and the discontent we feel. We are uncomfortable being still, so our mind is always in movement. Usually, we are not aware of this. We have explored the nature of pleasure and the fact that it is fleeting. Once we acquire something, the happiness fades. This may explain why we take what we already have for granted – because it no longer provides any stimulation or pleasure. Objects that bolster our sense of identity give us pleasure for a while longer. It is no longer just a car; it becomes 'my' car. Eventually, everything loses its appeal, with children and close relationships perhaps being an exception.

Another mechanism that may be involved is the unconscious process of comparison, which we have explored. Our mind looks at a landscape, a person, or an object, and compares what it sees with its memory bank. If it has seen it before, it does not register it freshly. This is one of the ways in which it organises itself most efficiently, so it only registers the new, or a possible danger, or a possible source of fresh stimulation. If we can become aware of this unconscious process at work, perhaps we could look at our world with fresh eyes and discover the extraordinary in our seemingly ordinary lives.

How can we respond to this fact with intelligence? The first step is to recognise this process at work in our lives. It operates behind the screen of our awareness.

Most of us have a lot to be thankful for. Particularly in times of great stress or even otherwise, it is worth reminding ourselves of all the things we can appreciate about our lives. My list includes my children, being moved by beauty, the poetry of Mary Oliver, having my health, the ability to run a 5k in my fifties, knowing people I love and who love me, having a deep connection with nature, and so on. What is on your list? Make one and add to it as you go. It is a real exercise in gratitude for all the things we have that we take for granted, and a bulwark against the anguish of stress that can make us *zoom in* on a problem and forget all that we still have to be thankful for.

Here is another exercise to try. Look around your home and think about the people in your life. Now notice them with fresh eyes, as if you are seeing them for the first time. Leave old memories and images behind. Be curious. Notice the small details you would usually overlook. Notice all the things you typically take for granted. Look again, admiring the best in people around you. Now step outdoors, looking at the flowers that you take for granted. Notice their details and their intricate, amazing beauty. Lie on the ground and look at the sky. Let its vastness soak in. See all the details of the clouds and their amazing formations, notice how quickly the landscape of the sky changes.

A combination of zooming out and being thankful puts all our problems and stresses into perspective. There is so much to be grateful for in our lives, if we can look with fresh eyes, without our memories of yesterday, and with a mind that is comfortable being in the present. Being aware of the mind's restlessness and search for pleasure brings us back to the present.

Do not escape

Stress is like a fire in the brain and our first instinct, as with all fires, is to run away from it. We do not know how to deal with it.

Our minds are inventive, and we probably have several well-worn patterns of distracting ourselves, many of which can lead to even greater problems than the stress that we are escaping from, though we do not realise that when we first set out on that road.

Alcohol dulls our senses and is commonly used to deal with stress. There is already a culture of drinking in the society we live in, and we may just gradually start drinking some more. A glass of wine becomes a bottle a day, a few beers become a few dozen, and so on. Because the emotional pain returns as soon as we stop drinking, we just continue. We discover that over time, we need to drink even more to get the same effect of dulling our senses. Any thought that it is bad for us and we should stop is quickly squashed by our inner urge for more, our urge to escape, and our habitual excuses. Before we know it, we have become dependent on alcohol.

Drug abuse is another way in which we can distract ourselves from our emotional pain. The dopamine released by opioid drugs dulls the emotional pain we are feeling. Any thoughts warning us of the dangers of taking drugs are silenced by our urge to get away from that feeling of stress. Nobody starts taking drugs thinking that they will end up addicted to them. Every drug addict whom I have spoken to felt that they could control the habit when they first started. Before we know it, we have become addicted to the drug, whatever it may be. The 67,000 deaths in 2018 in the US from drug overdoses reflects the scale of the problem. The numbers are similarly alarming around the world.

How much of the drug and alcohol problem in society is caused by people escaping from emotional pain? If 70–80% of the population reports significant stress, then it probably plays a major role, though exact data is not available. If we could educate everyone about stress, how to avoid it, and meet it with intelligence, it may reduce the problems caused by drug and alcohol consumption.

I have met several people whose journey to alcoholism or drug abuse started with an initial stressful event, and over the years, ended up destroying their health and the fabric of their lives. Sometimes people attempted to take their own lives. Any addiction leads to mental illness and diminishes our coping skills, making us more prone to stress and more vulnerable to harming ourselves.

Distraction through some form of pleasure is perhaps less harmful, and we have many ways in which we can do that. Going shopping and buying things brings comfort, even though it is short-lived. Often, we end up buying things that we do not need, and this contributes to debt and over-consumption.

Escaping from our emotional pain is not wrong, but it may not be the most intelligent thing to do. Since the fundamental cause of the pain is not understood, it will only continue to trouble us. The more we try to run from it, the more it will seem to follow us, and we cannot shake it off.

If instead we can stop, turn around and face it, we can find out where the fire began and put it out at its source. We can understand the root of stress in our thinking and employ the different strategies that we are exploring in this section to deal with our pain with a successful strategy instead.

If we allow the emotional pain to wash over us and face it entirely with stillness, meet it without thinking, as we will explore later, it transforms. In practice, this could mean sitting down somewhere comfortably, closing one's eyes, being present through a breathing exercise, and just being aware of the pain – without shirking or flinching from it, or engaging with it in any way. It rises and then falls away. The other advantage is that we can avoid the many problems that escaping from our stress can cause.

EVERYTHING PASSES

Every sorrow, like every storm, eventually passes. No matter how severe our psychological pain or disappointment, it ultimately fades from our memory. We just need to be patient and remain calm inside.

My parents were caught up in the horrors that followed the partition of India and Pakistan in 1947. Unspeakable acts of violence were committed by people on both sides of the divide. Neighbours who had lived peacefully for decades turned on each other. At the time they said that they did not think that they would ever get over it, but it passed, life renewed itself, and they moved on. They never spoke about it again. When asked directly about what happened, they would just say that there was no point going back and revisiting those events. I have seen similar reports from survivors of the Holocaust and other conflicts in the world.

At the time of the event, the psychological pain can seem visceral and take our breath away. Our mind just cannot imagine a time when this pain will not be there. On occasions like this, it is worth reminding ourselves that no pain lasts forever. The mind, like life itself, has a way of renewing itself. We just need to do the next thing that needs to be done and then the next one after that and keep going, giving our complete attention to living the life we have. All wounds heal and though the scars remain, as on our skin, they no longer cause pain, and after a while, we stop noticing them. We need to do our bit though and leave the past where it is. Perhaps we also need to practice compassion and forgiveness for this to happen. If a painful memory is triggered, we meet it without language.

We do have one thing we can do to help the healing along, and that is not to hang on to all our hurts and let them go. Otherwise, they fester and continue to hurt us all our lives. This requires us to understand our sense of identity, how it is formed, and how it makes us get attached to all our memories of pain.

There are, of course, serious psychological traumas that do not fall into this category, like PTSD, and people so afflicted need professional help.

IS THERE ANOTHER WAY TO SEE THE SAME SITUATION?

Once you have slowed the initial reaction down or got past it, you can ask if there is another way to see the same situation, perhaps from the other person's point of view. Our initial reaction comes from our particular slice of conditioning and it carries with it a certainty that we are correct. The intelligent response, therefore, is to ask ourselves if there is another way to see the same situation. That opens up options for the mind to consider, which it may not have otherwise. It may be that your initial view is still correct, but equally possible that you may discover new perspectives, many of which will not involve feeling stressed.

For example, if my friend does not call me as he said he would, I may be upset. But if I pause to consider other perspectives, they may include: he has lost his phone, or it has run out of power, or he is unwell, or has another problem to deal with. It may not mean that he does not care about me anymore. As my perspective changes, my stress disappears.

Or, if my boss sends me an email to come and see him the next day, I may lie awake at night wondering if I have done something wrong, or worse, if I am going to lose my job. When I pause and ask the question, other possibilities open up. He may be wanting to offer me a new responsibility, or congratulate me on something, or ask for my advice on something, and my stress eases.

If you are feeling insecure, and your husband has a work-related meeting with a woman, you may become suspicious that he is having an affair, and the anxiety of that may eat away at you. You do not want to confront him about it because that would reveal your own insecurity, but at the same time, you cannot get the idea out of your head. It lingers on, your stress and insecurity increase, affecting your relationship. If you asked yourself if there was another way of looking at the same situation, you might accept that you need to trust him and give him his freedom to meet the people he needs to meet. You may also look at your relationship and realise that it is in good shape. Finally, you may completely accept that it is a free world, and though you are married to him, you do not hold him in prison. On the rare chance that he does decide to end the relationship and move on, you will deal with it if it happens. By considering these options, your stress could dissolve.

All our relationships would be much healthier if we could consciously look at things from other people's perspectives, rather than exclusively our own.

It is not easy to ask if there is another way of seeing the same situation, especially in the midst of a storm in the mind where we feel certain that we are correct. Yet, it is a vital question to ask because it allows us to respond from a wider perspective and with intelligence.

Is THERE ANOTHER WAY TO RESPOND?

This seems like a natural question to follow the previous one. If I can see the same situation in different ways, I can also ask if there is another way to respond. My first response is reactive from my particular bit of conditioning, and we have explored how the reactive mind is not intelligent.

If you are talking to me about your views on a political leader, for example, and they are very different from mine, I may get angry, interrupt you, and try and convince you that you are wrong. We get into an argument that gets quite heated. If I can pause, I can ask myself if I can see things from your point of view and perhaps ask you a question about what shaped your opinion. The ability to listen well, without interrupting, is such a useful skill to have, but to do that, we need to be able to observe and slow our reaction down and explore other ways of responding.

My typical responses follow a pattern. If I usually get angry quickly, then the smallest incident will result in my anger flaring up. If, at the moment when it flares up, I can consider a different way to respond, I may lower my voice, soften my tone, ask a question, or say nothing. I can reflect on what effect my anger is going to have and whether it is going to help me achieve my goals. I may decide to wait and discuss the issue later when I have calmed down.

I was lecturing in a university and talking about our reactive mind. A young man in the audience stood up and said that he had got into trouble with the authorities since his school days because he was too quick to react and get angry. I asked him to give an example and he said that if he held the door open for someone and they did not say, "thank you", he would get angry and usually swear at them. He had the same response while driving. He had no insight into what was going on, so the pattern kept repeating itself. We talked about the origins of this reactive behaviour and how, asking if there was a different way to respond, would give him options to consider in the future. I met him several months later and he said that this insight had helped him.

When someone is irritated at something we have done, our instinctive reaction is to become defensive and angry, either justify ourselves or attack the other person back. If we can become conscious of the reaction occurring, we can respond in different ways. We may end up saying nothing and this may catch the other person off guard as they are expecting us to try and win the argument. Or we may stay calm and ask them why they think that way. We could also thank the person for their feedback and say that we are going to consider it. That usually defuses the situation and allows us to reflect if there is something we could learn from their criticism.

Exploring the different ways in which I can respond usually allows me to stay calm in a crisis and find creative ways to deal with the challenge at hand.

Is it in my zone of control?

In our age of the instant news cycle wherein events from across the globe flash across our screens as soon as they occur, all the bad news can make us feel depressed and stressed. It could be the climate crisis which seems to have no solution, or the wars in the world, or children starving in a famine, or the state of a country and its corrupt politics – the list is endless. We often get stressed about situations that are entirely outside of our influence. This question may allow you to reconsider your response.

In all these instances, it is worth asking if the thing that is stressing you out is in your 'zone of control'. If it is not, is there any point worrying about it? We know that good stories never make the news anyway. If we cannot do anything about 'it' (fill in the blank), how can we respond with intelligence? We still care, still want to know what is happening, and will do what we can in response, but we may refuse to let that situation cast a shadow over the life we are living right now.

This is also true of events and people closer to home. We cannot change the opinions, prejudices, or actions of people around us, but only our reactions to them. We can challenge their views when appropriate, but not expect them to change, as that can lead to disappointment. We cannot change the attitude and behaviour of our boss at work either, but only how we respond.

This question does not imply fatalistic pacifism wherein I accept injustice and do nothing. Consider the climate crisis. I do not let it get me stressed or depressed because I cannot change the big picture, nor do I hide away and pretend it is not happening. I do what I can in my own life. I reduce my consumption, take fewer trips away, recycle things, am vegetarian, and so on.

If I find myself consumed by worries, I can ask if they are in my *zone of control*, and if they are not, just let them go.

Are you attached to your own narrative?

We all become unconsciously attached to the stories we tell ourselves and to our opinions and beliefs, and when they are challenged or when people do not agree with us, we can get stressed. We have explored how this happens. The other person is attached to their narrative and before we know it, an argument has begun with each person digging in and giving reasons why they are correct. Conflict follows.

This attachment to our narrative can range from the smallest domestic issue, like how often the house needs cleaning, to bigger problems like what to do about the climate crisis.

The intelligent mind therefore asks, *"Am I attached to my narrative?"* No amount of repeating yourself or raising your voice is going to shift another person's point of view, and you will likely not allow your own view to be changed. So, what is the intelligent way to respond? Is your attachment to your point of view the cause of your distress?

The first step to alleviating this stress is to become aware of what is happening because it may not be obvious. You can then explore the situation from different points of view, without being attached to your own. This may encourage the other person to do the same. Or, you may realise that there is no point in engaging in a discussion because the other person is so attached to their point of view and you may just choose to keep quiet. You may also say something like, "It looks like we are both attached to our own points of view and are being reactive", and ask to continue the discussion later.

You may also realise that your attachment to your perspective stops you from learning anything new and you are the poorer for that. What is to be gained from getting the other person to agree with you?

If you do come across a person who has a point of view that you strongly disagree with, perhaps with a deep-seated prejudice (for example), what can you say to them? You could begin by realising that everyone is attached to their own point of view, so a direct approach is unlikely to work, and will instead, result in a backlash. If you seek to change their opinion, it may result in just reinforcing it. A more intelligent approach is needed. You could ask an open question such as, "Where do your opinions come from?" Or you could say, "We seem to have very differing views on this issue. I wonder how that came about?" That may open the door to a shared enquiry. Or you could listen deeply, without contradicting or interrupting. A person who feels deeply listened to is more likely to be open.

In any discussion which is generating heat, conflict, and stress, these are some useful questions to ask. They immediately open up other options for us to consider and our stress can dissolve. It can also allow us to learn something new.

ACCEPTANCE DISSOLVES STRESS

Stress is a disturbance in our thinking caused by the difference between how things are and how we want them to be or between who we are and who we want to be. This comes from our unconscious conditioning influences and we are not aware of this process at work in our lives. Our conscious mind just experiences stress and thinks that the cause of it is out there or in who we are.

If stress is the difference between how things are and how we want them to be, it follows that if we can accept things as they are, our stress can dissolve. Considering this possibility feels counter-intuitive for our mind, which does not see the unconscious process at work and is sure that the solution lies in changing the person or the situation in front of us. We can change that sometimes, but not often. If we can become aware of the unconscious process at work behind the scenes, we can ask ourselves if we can accept things as they are, and if we can, then our stress can finish right there. As I have said, it is simple, but not easy.

I met a teacher who had been off work with stress, which she felt was caused by too much work. She was convinced that it was the workload that was causing her stress. We explored the possibility that it was her reaction to the workload that was causing her stress and I asked if there was another way of seeing the same situation. We also explored acceptance, that is, if it was possible for her to accept the situation as it was and do the best that she could. She had never considered acceptance as a reasonable response, and once she did, she said her stress went away and she returned to work.

This acceptance can help dissolve much of the stress we experience in our day-to-day life. If I can accept that your opinion is different from mine, or so is your gender preference, your skin colour, your religion, or the way you stack the dishwasher, or the fact that my son does not call as often as I want, my stress dissolves right there. Try this. Make a list of the common things that cause repeated stress and ask if you can accept them as they are.

What did you discover?

The same principle of acceptance applies to the stress caused by the difference between who I am and who I want to be – my many ideals. Say I am a young man and want to look more muscular, or be smarter, or be the perfect father, and so on. I worry what others are thinking of me, I think I am not good enough, and try to change. If I cannot match my ideal, I feel stressed. This process can also rob me of my self-esteem, make me anxious, and push me to conform to be someone else. I am sure that the problem lies in who I am and do not see that the actual problem lies in my ideal of who I want to be, which comes from my unconscious conditioning influences. I just think that my looks are stressing me out or the fact that I am not as popular or as wealthy as I want to be. I have a perfect image of myself that I am chasing and since I cannot do much about how I look, for example, I am likely to be always stressed.

I ask myself, "How can I respond to this fact with intelligence?" It becomes clear to me – like seeing a deep blue sky on a sunny day – that the answer lies in accepting myself as I am. I uncover and then let go of all the unconscious images that were causing my stress (like being the perfect parent), and I find that my stress dissolves. Paradoxically, I find that if I can accept myself as I am, others are more likely to do so as well because I am much more relaxed and happier as a person.

It is this acceptance that allows people to move on from their disabilities, for example, and make the most of the life they have. I know a man who is paraplegic and goes hang-gliding. Or, look at the athletes competing in the Paralympics.

This understanding may, for example, help young men and women avoid eating disorders because of anxiety about how they look. About 1.6 million people in Britain suffer from an eating disorder. One of the well-known eating disorders is Anorexia Nervosa and mortality rates from it are as high as 20%. It has the highest mortality of all the mental health disorders and it has its roots in body-image and control issues. Acceptance of ourselves as we are can perhaps help us avoid and overcome this.

I am not suggesting that this acceptance can apply to every situation and there are situations which are impossible to accept. It wever, asking oneself these questions:

- Can I accept things as they are?
- Is my unconscious conditioning contributing to the stress I feel?
- Can I explore and let go of my images of who I should or want to be?
- Can I accept myself as I am?

Ask yourself these questions and see what emerges. Challenge yourself even if it feels hard. You may be surprised at what you discover. To do this, we have to let go of our sense of right and wrong because that blocks enquiry. We also need to question our certainties because they are created by a trick of our thinking. If you can accept things as they are, your stress could end. It may not require any effort either. Making the unconscious conscious, allows intelligence to operate, and that can bring change without effort.

Acceptance does not mean that you stop trying to change a situation that needs changing. Acceptance means you can do it with a calm mind.

"I CAN GET THROUGH THIS" – A POSITIVE ATTITUDE

Stress diminishes our capacity to cope with it, so a positive attitude is useful in addressing the challenge and getting through it. Amid our suffering, we can remind ourselves that we have an enormous capacity to overcome the difficulties in our lives, even when faced with untold hardship. There are many stories of people who have overcome adversity to shine in their lives. We see them after they have become successful or famous, but please pause to think of the crisis they faced and the positive energy they summoned within themselves to keep going. We can do the same.

Franklin D. Roosevelt was paralysed from the waist down by polio but overcame that to become president of the United States, four times. Maya Angelou, the poet and writer, overcame so much adversity as a child, to give to the world the gift of her poems and books. Albert Einstein did not have a job for two years before eventually getting one as a patent clerk. Soldiers in all wars face so much horror and adversity, but find a way of moving past that. Each of us is different and will recover at different times from life's challenges, but a positive attitude certainly helps.

In the midst of a stressful situation, what can you do? It may help to focus on possible solutions rather than the problem. Ask yourself, "*How can I...?*", rather than think of the reasons why nothing can be done. Even if you take a small step towards accepting and solving a problem, you will find the energy to keep going.

If you demand the best of yourself, have a positive attitude, and say, "I am going to get through this", you will find reservoirs of energy that you did not know existed. Sometimes there may be no solution possible and you just have to endure the situation. Here, I am thinking of prisoners of war or refugees or an illness. The inner strength to endure comes if we have a positive attitude and demand the best from ourselves.

On the other hand, what does it look like to have a negative attitude? The word 'negative' is part of our language and I wish there was another word I could use that did not imply judgement. This is a common way in which our mind responds to adversity and is not anyone's fault, but just the way our mind works.

I say this with kindness and mean no criticism; perhaps having a negative attitude implies that we see the worst in a situation and imagine the worst scenario going forwards. We think people have acted out of deliberate malice towards us when they may not have. We regard ourselves as victims and complain ceaselessly about what has happened to us. We keep going over events that have already happened, rather than focusing on the present and what needs to be done next. We never ask ourselves if we may, in some way, be responsible for our reaction to the event or for what happened, for example, if we were in a relationship that failed. We do not see any solution going forwards and believe that nothing can change. We have no hope for the future. If you spot this attitude in yourself and can say, "Come on! You can be better than this", an amazing thing happens. You find the energy to deal with the challenge you are facing and look at things more positively. This gives you the best chance of overcoming adversity and moving on.

Having a positive attitude is something we have to teach ourselves ...se it does not always come naturally. Start with simple things. ;on you do not like and think of a positive way to see the When you find yourself being critical of someone, pause)est in them. If you are in a job you dislike, ask yourself how having a positive attitude could change your perspective of it. If you practice in small ways, it gradually becomes second nature, so when the big challenges of life arrive, you have the skills to navigate them.

TAKE RESPONSIBILITY FOR YOUR REACTIONS

For this journey of exploring our inner spaces, this is a crucial step. We know we need to take responsibility for our actions in the world, but we are less likely to consider taking responsibility for our feelings and emotional reactions. This is because the mechanism behind them is hidden from our awareness and we do not realise that they begin in our thinking.

For example, if I see a spider, react, and feel afraid, I think it is the spider that has made me afraid, but as we have explored, it is our own reaction that generates our fear. Or, if I am at work and feel that no one recognises my worth, I will feel bad and blame the organisation or my boss for how I feel. I do not realise that the need to feel important comes from me, as does my reaction.

Accepting that our reactions emerge from our thinking even though they are triggered by other people or events is not easy because the way in which our mind functions convinces us that others are the cause of our stress. We do not see the internal processes of thinking that are behind our reactions. That is hidden from us. We only see the external trigger. If we look more closely though, it is quite clear that stress is usually a reaction from our conditioned mind to the external event.

Taking responsibility for our feelings and our reactions has many benefits.

Firstly, it opens the door to learning more about where these reactions come from and what is behind them.

Secondly, it stops us from blaming others for how we feel. Blaming them could make us retaliate and hurt them, which can damage our relationships further. So much disharmony in our relationships could be avoided if we could do this.

Lastly, taking responsibility for our reactions means that we may feel empowered to do something about our own stress. We no longer have to depend on other people or situations to change for our stress to go away. We can change how we respond to those challenges, and that has the potential of ending our stress.

We have explored previously that our feelings and reactions are not right or wrong, or good or bad. They just are, and by taking responsibility for them, we can respond with intelligence.

We are talking here about our psychological reactions to events. There are many instances where this will not apply, for example, if we are physically abused in any way.

WHAT CAN I LEARN?

Of all the questions I ask myself when I am stressed, this one is my favourite because it opens the door to discovering something new about myself and the origins of stress in my own thinking.

Let me illustrate this with a hypothetical example. Say it is my wedding anniversary, and I take great care to prepare a card for my wife and buy her some gifts. On the morning of the anniversary, I surprise her with the card and present and she is delighted. I am, however, bitterly disappointed to find out that she has forgotten that it was our anniversary and not arranged any presents or card for me. The pain is searing and takes my breath away. I get angry with her and think of ways in which I can retaliate and hurt her back. Of course, it is her fault for upsetting me and stressing me out. How can there be another way of looking at it? To me, this is a sign that she does not really care about me or think that our relationship is important. There have been several other occasions when I have been disappointed with her and said nothing, but this time, all my anger comes spilling out.

If I pause, breathe, and follow the three steps to self-enquiry, I begin by observing that I am angry and upset with her. I stay with that feeling and realise that it is my own unmet expectation that is causing my pain. Accepting this is hard, but I do because it is a fact. I then ask myself this really important question, "What can I learn?" That opens the door to discovery. I learn that I have many unconscious expectations that I carry with me. I am only aware of these expectations when I feel the pain if they are not met. The implications for my life are many. I realise that is the reason why so many of my relationships get strained. I used to think that it was always the other person's fault, but now I realise that the root of the problem lies in my expectations. I am curious now and begin exploring further. Where do these expectations come from? Do they come from the society I grew up in? Are they my responsibility since they emerge from my thinking or are other people responsible for meeting my expectations? Can I live without them? By this point, my anger has subsided, and I am fascinated by what I am finding out about myself.

What began as a very stressful event has become a valuable learning opportunity. I have learnt about expectations and this understanding changes my life. I stop getting angry with others for not meeting these expectations, which I realise come from my conditioning and my emotional needs. These expectations are not wrong either. It is just the way the mind is wired. I stop being angry with my wife. I do tell her that I felt awful that she forgot our anniversary, but do not blame her for it. Instead, I share what I have learnt about myself. She apologises for forgetting our anniversary and makes amends. This opens the door for us to talk in more detail about our expectations and disappointments and how these can accumulate, gradually eroding our relationship. This dialogue is healthy, without blame, and does not result in a reaction from either of us. We end up feeling closer than before the episode began.

Every stressful situation becomes an occasion to understand how my mind works. I am continually learning from my reactions. As a result, the situations that trigger a stress reaction in me are fewer and fewer. Once I have learnt something, the same situation does not trigger the same reaction next time around. On some occasions, there is no stress at all.

Consider a second example. A work colleague has just bought a new house and posts pictures of it on social media. The house is beautiful and much larger than mine. I wonder how he can afford it. I immediately feel envious that others are better than me: have money, more interesting lives, and have more fun. Social media gradually makes me feel inferior to others, puts pressure on me to conform to an ideal, and I slowly lose my self-confidence.

I ask myself how I can respond to this with intelligence. I am curious as to what is happening inside me. I begin by observing that looking at social media is causing me to feel stressed and I blame others for how

I am feeling. Since the feeling arises in me, I decide to take responsibility for how I am feeling and ask myself what I can learn. I discover that my mind compares itself to others all the time and this happens unconsciously. I then observe the many other areas of my life where this comparison operates and notice that this feeling of envy comes up quite regularly. It seems that this reaction is not in my control, and even if I want to, I cannot stop being envious. In some areas, this comparison is essential, but in other areas, it is causing me a lot of stress. As I begin to observe the process of comparison operating in me, I ask myself if I can stop comparing myself to others. I am not sure exactly how it happens, but just noticing it each time changes something in me and I no longer feel envious of others. If envy does arise in me, I recognise the process behind it and it ends immediately. This understanding has other benefits. I find myself free to follow my own path in life because I no longer automatically compare myself to others.

This journey to be free of the stress caused by expectations and comparison began though with a simple question, "What can I learn from my stress?"

Meet stress without thinking

Please walk with me as we explore this idea that initially may seem quite strange. It seems that *everything* we do involves thinking, and why would we want to meet stress *without thinking,* anyway?

There are four reasons why this may be worth considering.

The first is that stress emerges from our thinking. It is a response from our conditioned, reactive mind to the world around us and the difference between what we see and what we know. The entire process involves thinking. Some thoughts are loud and easily noticed, others have a very low volume, are fleeting, and need an extraordinary sensitivity to observe. We have explored how we can nurture this sensitivity. If we can meet stress without thinking, we can cut off the oxygen to the thought process that started the fire and it can end of its own accord.

The second is that by not *naming* it as stress, we are able to *notice* in much greater depth and detail the mechanism behind our stress reaction. This could be comparison or pleasure or fear, for example. If you look at a landscape and say, "That is beautiful!", take a photograph, and move on, you have overlooked so much of the detail in it. As soon as we name something, we stop really looking at it. We need language to communicate what we think and feel, but we do not need language or thinking to *observe* what is happening in our inner spaces.

The third reason is that our mind responds to stress with a cascade of thoughts. Each thought then triggers other thoughts, and before we know it, we are overwhelmed by the sheer number of thoughts pulling us in different directions. We get confused by the 'smoke' these thoughts create and can lose our clarity about how to respond. If I am stressed because someone has become angry with me over something I have done, then various thoughts arise in response. Here is a sample of possible reactions:

- I think that it is the other person's fault for hurting me.
- I feel that I am right and justified in what I did.
- I say something negative about the other person.
- I think of ways to retaliate.
- I think that other people would agree with me and my response.
- I feel that I should be able to deal with criticism better and I am critical of myself.

Our many thoughts in response to stress can increase the distress and suffering we feel. We keep going over and over what was said, the pain we experienced, and how we can retaliate. It can also make us anxious about being shouted at in the future because this episode has been so painful. However, staying with the *fact* of someone being angry with us allows us to explore it further. We could then explore why the other person got angry, what the reaction in us is, why we react in a particular way, what is the entity that gets hurt, and so on.

Lastly, we have explored how the 'I' that experiences all the suffering is a construct of our thinking, though this is not easy to see. Even if we grasp the idea of this intellectually, it continues to operate because it is so hard-wired into our thinking from millennia of conditioning. If we can meet stress without thinking, then the 'I' that experiences all the stress is also no longer there to feel it, and that is another way in which stress can melt away.

Meeting something without thinking is a simple idea, but not easy to implement. To our mind that functions almost entirely through thinking, it may seem impossible. Again, please continue walking with me as we explore how we can meet stress or any other feeling, without thinking.

Try this exercise. Fill a glass of water and keep it on the table. When you first look at it, what do you see? Most people see water in a glass and stop looking further. Now, look at it a second time without consciously naming it and notice all the play of light in it. Notice the reflections and shadows and keep looking, noticing all the detail. Notice also the thoughts that arise in your mind. Do not push them to one side, but keep looking. Can you look at that glass of water without a single thought arising and coming in the way of that observation? If you keep looking and noticing both the glass and the thoughts that come and go, gradually your mind will become quiet, and you can see the glass without thinking, just noticing the play of light and shadow around it. After you have practised this exercise with a few objects, try and look at the feeling of stress in the same way. Stay with it, do not move away, and observe it without thinking. See what emerges.

You may feel frustrated if you cannot do this, to begin with. It is not easy for the mind to break a habit of a lifetime and see something without naming it or thinking about it. When we were children, the first thing we learnt was how to name things. Everything has a name. Language is embedded in our thinking. We lose the ability to look at things simply, with curiosity that we had as children. Start with simple things in the world outside, even if it is only for a minute. Keep going. Notice a sensation like hunger or thirst and observe it in this way. Or notice the urge that makes you pick up your phone or put the TV on and just stay with it, meeting it without language. See what happens. Gradually you will be able to see a sunrise, for example, without naming it, and that allows you to notice all its beauty. If you can look in this way, you will find that your mind becomes quiet in the process. In this quietude, you become aware of your own breathing and also notice the 'I' recording it all. Continue exploring the four dimensions of awareness that we discussed earlier.

Observing does not require language, only communicating does.

Do not allow stress to condition you

Life is full of unexpected challenges. Suffering is part of being human. Every experience that brings us pain gets stored in our memory and becomes part of our unconscious conditioning from which our mind reacts to the world. If I have been attacked by a snake, for example, I learn to recognise a poisonous one in the future and can avoid it. That is just intelligent. If, on the other hand, it creates in me a life-long fear of going for a walk in the woods and stops me from doing that, that is clearly not in my interest and may not be an intelligent response. My experience has conditioned my behaviour for the rest of my life, without my realising it.

I met a young man whose friend had been killed a year before. He was not sleeping, having nightmares, held himself responsible, and was withdrawn, morose, and depressed. He felt frightened that the same thing could happen to him or his other friends one day. His life was passing him by and he was living in the past. He could not change what had happened. Neither did he feel he could snap out of his low mood and depression. The event from a year ago had conditioned him, influenced his behaviour, and affected his mood. How could he move on and live freshly in the present?

A young woman has her heart broken by a man whom she trusted. She met him, fell in love, and wanted to build a future with him. They had been together for many years. He then had an affair and left her for the other woman. She was angry and upset with him and now finds it very difficult to trust anyone else or have an intimate relationship. She feels that he shattered her dreams for a happy family life and she does not know what to do.

A teacher is very anxious about a lesson evaluation that is coming up. He has been hurt by criticism before and this has conditioned him to get worried in case it ever happens again. Even the thought of criticism can set his anxiety going again. It shapes his behaviour and social interactions. He does not feel able to do anything about it and continues to suffer. Eventually, he leaves the teaching profession because he cannot cope with the stress of being judged by others.

These examples illustrate how we are conditioned by our stressful experiences, *without our awareness or our consent*. Given the option, do you think you would ever consent to being conditioned by your experiences? We suffer not only from the stress of the original event, but from the painful memory we carry all our lives and it shapes our thoughts and actions for the future.

How can we respond to this fact that we are conditioned by our stress, with intelligence? The first step is to notice how our stress subtly conditions us and then operates in the background, directing the course of our lives. Do we want our past to shape our future without our awareness or our consent? If we have been hurt before, do we want our future happiness to be blighted by that? Is it intelligent to think badly of an entire community of people because of the actions of a few? Suppose others hated us because people with our skin colour, religion, nationality, or gender had done something to hurt them? We would find that upsetting and say that it is not a rational or an intelligent response.

Once we become aware that stressful events in our past affect our thinking and actions in the present, what can we do to be free, if we want to be? Once the unconscious has been made conscious, then we have the choice to apply our intelligence and decide that we are not going to allow our past to condition our present and future because we can see the problems that it can cause. We cannot erase the past, but whenever it comes up, we meet it with intelligence and the understanding that it was an isolated incident in a long life. When I catch myself thinking about the past and reliving the stress I felt, I can meet that with intelligence too. I also see that hanging on to painful memories brings me a subtle pleasure from feeling like a victim. This seems to happen unconsciously and of its own accord. Instead, I just stop doing that and focus on the present. The cycle is broken. If, what happened in my past was a tragedy, it is multiplied many times over if I allow it to condition my future. I see that very clearly and that insight brings freedom. This freedom allows me to live with joy in the present, without fear, and meet life and people freshly.

Another insight that allows me to leave the past where it belongs (in the past) is acceptance of whatever happened, as we have explored, and through compassion and forgiveness.

HOW CAN WE DEAL WITH PAINFUL MEMORIES?

We have explored how our painful memories are kept alive by our thinking processes. Even years after a traumatic event, memories can be triggered by any association with that past action: something we read or listened to, or perhaps upon seeing a person or a picture. The memories come flooding back and can be powerful. It can feel like the event happened just yesterday. We react to that pain in common ways: withdraw, blame others, get angry, get depressed or anxious, or try to escape. These reactions can continue to influence our lives for many years, and affect our opinions, our behaviour, our aspirations, and our relationships. Sometimes our mind wants to hang on to these painful memories and not let them go, even though they are painful. They become woven into our identity of who we are. Some of us would like to get rid of them but do not know how. Our memories keep coming back to trouble us. What can we do?

We could begin by realising that they are not real. The only reality is the life we live right now, the breath we are taking, the apple we are eating, the person we are talking to. These painful memories stop us from enjoying the gift of life that we have been presented with.

I was watching a film the other day and a particular scene triggered a bitter-sweet memory from years ago. It was overpowering, like being hit by a powerful aroma as you walk past a kitchen. I sat down and let it flow through me without any resistance. I just watched it unfold. I did not name it and not a single thought arose as a response to it. The feeling reached a peak and then ebbed away. In the end, I was left with a sense of immense quietness, like a feeling of grace. The next time you find yourself similarly caught up in a memory by your senses, consider responding in this way and see how it might alter your relationship to that memory from your past.

We cannot get rid of our memories, even if we want to. But we could at least try to not hang on to them. Compassion and forgiveness can together help in loosening the hold unpleasant past experiences may have on our lives. Living with awareness also helps, so if a memory is triggered, we can respond with awareness – by allowing memories to rise in us without resistance, observing them without engagement, and letting them go. This method allows us to return our attention to the present. The more you practise moving through life this way, the more it can become second nature.

COMPASSION AND FORGIVENESS

There are many occasions in life where we feel that others have behaved badly towards us and we blame them for our stress and hurt. We keep thinking about what happened and have a sense of injustice. This keeps our pain alive. We tell our friends our story of what happened and how we were wronged. They agree with us and sympathise, and this strengthens our narrative. There is nothing right or wrong about this. It is just the way our mind works.

Or, we may blame ourselves for something we did in the past and feel guilty.

How can we respond to this with intelligence? It is clear that our stress and anger harms us more than anyone else, so what can we do to move on? We know that acceptance dissolves stress, but how can we accept when we feel we have been so terribly wronged and the other person has behaved so badly?

This requires compassion and forgiveness. *Compassion* is a feeling of goodness for others and oneself, and comes from empathy and understanding that the human mind functions in the same way in all of us and deep down we are all the same human being. *Forgiveness* is to let go of any ill will that we may harbour for others and oneself for things that we or others have done that were harmful and which we regard as wrong.

What will awaken these feelings of compassion and forgiveness in us? Say you have been wronged, are deeply hurt, and are churning away inside. How can you possibly forgive? Someone comes along and tells us, "*Forgiveness is for your own benefit*" and we should "*Forgive and move on*". All the religions have said so. Even if you accept that idea, you may not know how to forgive someone, even if you want to. It remains an idea, an unattainable goal, and your inner churn, anger, and distress continue. How do you begin?

You could start by seeing the importance of this for your own well-being. You see that your anger and stress is harming you, mentally and physically, and this new self-awareness gives you the energy to investigate further. As we have explored, change comes from exploring facts, not from pursuing ideals. Exploring the fact, in this case, is to try and understand what is behind your feeling of being hurt and behind the behaviour of others. We rarely do this. Instead we either react with anger or create the ideal of forgiveness that we try and pursue. Because the deeper causes of our hurt have not been understood, the ill-feeling in us does not entirely go away, making forgiveness difficult, even if we want to.

The first step on a road of compassion and forgiveness is to gain insight into the motivations behind the behaviour of others, especially those that we feel have done us harm. So, you may ask, "*What drives people to act in the way they do?*" There are many factors, but here are five to consider.

The first is conditioning. All unconscious past experiences are stored in our memory, and that determines opinions and behaviour. I am the same. So are you.

The second is the fulfilment of hidden inner needs. People need to feel important, secure, listened to, understood, connected to others, have power, pleasure, be able to speak about themselves, be wealthy, live without conflict, and so on. I am the same. So are you.

The third is self-interest. Their self-interest operates in the background, pushing them to get their emotional and physical needs met, and this urge is so powerful that it sometimes overlooks the needs or feelings of others. I am the same. So are you.

The fourth is fear. Unconscious fears of the future, of being attacked, being lonely, being poor, being a nobody, or becoming ill, shape opinions and behaviour. I am the same. So are you.

The fifth is our reaction to a feeling of being hurt. This feeling of being hurt makes us react with anger and say and do things that are irrational and hurt others. We have little control over such reactions because they are so powerful. I am the same. So are you.

Behind the screen of our awareness, all of us human beings are the same. The same processes of thinking operate in all of us. It does not mean that we are not responsible and accountable for our actions. But it can awaken compassion in each of us. If we are two smokers in a smoking shelter, I will not blame you for smoking because we are the same. I will only be critical of you if I think you are different. I see that most people are not aware of the many hidden forces that direct their behaviour, and I am no different, so how can I be critical of them? Yes, they did something that hurt me, but they acted mostly from ignorance rather than malice. That understanding awakens compassion, which leads to forgiveness. I did not start out to forgive, but merely to understand. Compassion and forgiveness arise naturally as a by-product of that understanding. Once this understanding arises within, it seems to require no effort. Gradually the memory of the pain that I felt also washes away and I am free. This freedom is within the grasp of all human beings, including you, and me.

The same process of compassion also applies to ourselves. We all may have done things we later regret. The same unconscious need for pleasure and security, which operates in all human beings, also operates in us. This urge to fulfil our inner needs is so strong that it overrides any thought that comes in the way. This is not to excuse our behaviour, but an attempt to understand the origins of it in our thinking. We may learn something from that, which may help us in the future. It also allows us to have compassion towards ourselves and forgive ourselves for things we may have done, which we regret. This allows us to learn from our mistakes and move on with our lives, live fully in the present, make amends if we can, and live with compassion and intelligence.

There are so many examples of people who have applied this understanding to forgive others in the most challenging circumstances. Let me share some stories which struck me.

Bassam Aramin was 17 when he was imprisoned for seven years for throwing stones at an Israeli jeep, and later beaten while in prison. On his release, under the Oslo peace accord, he married and had a family. His ten-year-old daughter was killed by an Israeli soldier. Though his suffering was incalculable, he refused to respond with hatred and revenge and instead chose to forgive saying, "Forgiveness is in the first place for yourself and your own healing. It is a way of life. It is a way to clean your heart and make peace with yourself. It is refusing to be a victim". Elik Elhanan was an Israeli soldier whose sister was killed by a suicide bomb in Jerusalem. He also chose to forgive and, with Bassam, formed an organisation that works to end the conflict in the region. There are many similar stories from the decades of conflict in the area.

Nelson Mandela was imprisoned for 27 years by the apartheid regime in South Africa but went on to forgive his oppressors, become president, and unite the country around a new shared vision. He said, "Forgiveness liberates the soul, it removes fear". He also said, "...the most difficult task in life is changing yourself".

Many stories go unnoticed: like the man who forgave his wife for having an affair and breaking his heart or the woman who forgave the driver of the car that killed her son.

I met a lady who said that understanding why people behave the way they do had helped her forgive her parents. They had refused to accept her boyfriend who was a different skin colour to them, and this had caused a lot of heartache. She now understood that they were just acting from their unconscious conditioning and were not aware that they were doing so. There is an unhappy memory in most of us that this process can help release and allow us to be free to live richly in the present.

These and other examples can inspire us to go beyond our instinctive reactions to being hurt and be the best versions of ourselves that we can be. We need to dig deep, understand ourselves and others, and from that understanding emerges a spring of goodness that can nourish our own lives, heal our hurts, forgive others, and inspire others to do the same.

Get help

In the middle of an emotional crisis, the mind loses its ability to see and think clearly. It does not know how to get out of its cage of misery. It is at times like these that it is essential to get professional help. There is no stigma attached to this. It is so much better to do this early on. A mixture of talking therapy and medication is often effective in treating depression or anxiety.

In my view, this needs to be combined with self-understanding and exploring the origins of stress in our thinking. Medication can help manage the symptoms but does not treat the root cause of our stress, which often originates in our thinking.

The person who is stressed not only does not know that he needs help, but also refuses help when it is offered because it is seen as a 'stigma' or a sign of 'weakness', particularly among men.

It is also useful to be able to speak to our closest friends and family members and share what is going on in our inner spaces. Sometimes just talking about our distress and getting a fresh perspective can help unlock our understanding and make us feel better. For many of us, this feels like a challenge, and we are afraid of how people will respond. It may help us to realise that our stress is not unique to us, but is a feeling shared by all human beings. Opening up to others may encourage them to be more open with us, and that may deepen and strengthen our relationships.

MAKE PEACE WITH YOUR INNER BOREDOM

We have explored through this book how our inner restlessness, boredom, or sense of feeling empty or dissatisfied can drive our thoughts and actions. This feeling is at the core of our consciousness or the way our mind works, and is shared among all human beings.

It gives rise to our feeling of loneliness when there is no person with whom we can connect and our need to speak and be understood is not met. This feeling causes so much distress.

It is behind our feeling of boredom when we feel that there is nothing to do. This feeling of boredom often prompts us to take alcohol or drugs, and because it never goes away, we need more and more to get the same effect. We have explored all the damage this can cause.

All our journeys to seek pleasure begin from this feeling in an attempt to move away from it. We are usually not aware of this. Many of these journeys end in stress and disappointment, but we do not see the connection between the two.

This is also where our need to feel important comes from. In all our activities we try subtly to get others to make us feel important, whether at home or in the organisations we are in. When this is not met or we are displaced from our position of authority, we feel hurt.

Many of our long list of emotional needs also have their origins in this feeling because when they are met, we think that the feeling goes away.

It is behind the smartphone addiction that has spread everywhere in the world. It is what prompts us to pick up the phone when there is no reason to.

It also drives our attachment to our various identities and beliefs because they meet our needs for security and pleasure. Such attachments can cause stress and conflict.

None of the above makes the feeling of inner emptiness disappear. It is just covered up and remains under the surface, still operating in the background.

Our inner boredom or emptiness is not wrong. At present, though, this emptiness operates unconsciously, hidden from our awareness, directing our lives in a variety of ways. Becoming aware of this feeling allows us to make our peace with it and respond with wisdom.

How can we respond with wisdom to this feeling that we all have?

The first step, as always, is to become aware of the ache of that feeling of emptiness in us without naming it or judging it or justifying it. Just get curious about it. Observe how this emptiness operates in the background and notice all the different ways in which it works in our life. Noticing does not require language. Notice how this inner boredom makes us uncomfortable and want to move away from it by thinking or doing something. Just stay with that feeling, allowing it to be. Staying with it is not easy because our mind has a well-established habit of escaping from it. If you do get distracted, do not worry, it will be there again soon.

If you do manage to stay with that feeling of inner boredom, which we experience as an inner ache, allowing it to be, without naming it or judging it or escaping from it, it transforms into a sense of peace. This peace is the deepest desire we all have but has eluded the human heart for millennia. It is not to be found in the world outside but inside us. Our journey, which began with a question, trying to understand the root cause of stress, has culminated in the discovery of a sense of peace. May you discover it too.

LETTER TO A FRIEND

Dear Reader,

It is now winter. As I sit at my desk, there are just a few dozen leaves left on the oak tree in front of my window. They seem to be clinging on, but they will also soon be gone. There is a naked beauty in seeing the architecture of a tree with its intricate shape. There is a similar beauty in being a simple human being, without any attachment to our various identities. I have been writing for ten months. When I started, I had no idea of the shape the book would take or the ideas that would flow from the exploration of stress. Writing the book has changed me, and I hope that reading it has done the same for you.

Of all the things I have written about, the most significant step for me was to start taking responsibility for my thoughts and feelings and asking what I could learn about myself by exploring them. That opened the door to so many discoveries. As a result, much of the ordinary stress of day-to-day life has just melted away. For example, seeing the problems caused by comparing myself to others, and then no longer doing that, has seen the ache of envy just disappear.

The other significant revelation was that *how* I looked at myself was the key to the discoveries that I made and that is why I have explored that extensively. To explore our inner spaces, we need a different way of looking and it is worth getting that right before we begin. It requires an idle curiosity, an interest, and a way of noticing without naming or judging what we find. This exploration of our inner spaces is not an intellectual affair. If we make it one, we may become clever, but our heart remains unchanged.

What challenges did you face when exploring your inner spaces? You and I are the same human being, so that landscape is the same in both of us. This fact allowed me to accept myself as I am. We think that we are unique because we look different and the content of our memory is unique, but that is just a small part of who we are. Were you tempted to give up? Does it all seem too complicated? This approach is simple, but not easy. All we need is curiosity, a spirit of learning, and an open mind. It does not need intellectual capacity. All we are doing is observing the way in which our shared human mind works and then applying that learning to our lives. We need to begin with the content of our memory, but not get stuck there, analysing things. We need to move quickly beyond that to explore the hidden processes of thinking that operate beyond the screen of our awareness, and then explore the nature of the 'I' itself. This is the same in all human beings. That understanding brings freedom.

Did this journey awaken in you a sense of compassion? It has done in me. This compassion, once awakened, extends beyond the people and things we identify with as ours. When I meet another human being, I see that deep down, we are the same, not as an *idea*, but as a *fact*. That is a crucial difference.

I have an important question to ask you. What are you going to do with this wisdom that you have discovered in yourself? Are you going to be a force for good in the world or just use it for your own benefit? The human mind is so capable and so focused on its self-interest that it can turn everything into an opportunity for its own benefit. It does this unconsciously, but by being aware of this process, we can respond with goodness. There is so much unnecessary suffering in the world. What are you going to do about that? Are you going to try, in your own small way, to make the world a better place?

A surprising discovery was that a journey that began in trying to uncover the origins of stress, resulted in discovering a sense of peace. Did you find that too? It is not a goal to be arrived at or an achievement, but a natural by-product of this enquiry. It is not a destination, but something that is discovered freshly every day.

I started this journey, thinking that stress is a problem to be solved, but instead, it became an opportunity to learn about myself and how my mind works. Our stress reactions emerge from our inner spaces, so are also a window into understanding our inner landscape. It is when we are afraid that we can study the feeling and understand the nature of fear. It is when we are envious that we learn that the mind is comparing all the time, and so on. These discoveries have transformed my life. I hope that they have changed yours too in some way. Do not be disappointed if they have not. Please keep going. Learning the piano takes patience and perseverance, as does climbing any mountain.

If you discover something beautiful, you want to share it with others. How could you help take this to a wider audience so that others too could avoid so much unnecessary stress in their lives? To bring this understanding to a wider audience, especially in education, I set up the Human Wisdom Project. You can find out more at humanwisdom.me and follow the project on social media.

The beauty of this approach is that it is like looking at the moon together and sharing what we discover. No person discovered the moon and no one owns it. It was there all along, available for anyone with curiosity to explore. Similarly, we are just exploring the mind that we all share, not according to anyone's ideas, but as it is. As a result, there is no need for any authority. Anything I have said in this book is only true if you see it for yourself. This understanding of ourselves and how our mind works awakens our inner intelligence, which can transform our life. If you change, the world changes. You can be your own teacher.

Go gently. Discover wisdom. Find peace.

Manoj Krishna

GLOSSARY OF TERMS

I HAVE USED A NUMBER of everyday words sometimes in new ways, and I thought it would be helpful to explore their meanings in a bit more detail for the curious reader.

Awareness: this includes not just what we receive with our senses, but also noticing our thoughts and feelings.

The Mind: is the way our thought processes are organised. It is the software to the brain's hardware.

Intelligence/Intelligent mind: refers to a mind that lives with awareness and self-understanding, not only of the content of its memory, but also an understanding of the many processes of thinking like conditioning, images, etc.

Inner intelligence: is similar to the above, but used to differentiate it from intellect, which you could use to refer to someone who was smart, capable, and scored high marks in the exams.

Vibrant intelligence: a term I use to indicate that this inner intelligence is ALIVE, vibrant, full of energy and vitality, and not a dull, passive entity.

Reactive mind: refers to the process of thinking whereby an external stimulus triggers an automatic reaction from our memory. This reaction comes from a tiny part of that memory. For example, if you are at a dinner, and the conversation turns to train journeys, you will begin talking about your favourite train journey, and not even be aware of this. Or, if you come across something very different from what you are used to, for example, a gay couple kissing, you will have an instant negative reaction. Not all our reactions are expressed and we usually have varying degrees of self-control, based on the situation.

Conditioned mind: is a mind that has been influenced by all its past experiences and by its environment but usually has no awareness that this has happened. This conditioning shapes our thoughts and actions.

Meditative mind: is a mind that is self-aware and carries this awareness through the day. This awareness includes whatever is happening outside in the world and in the world inside, and includes a quality of silence.

Making the unconscious conscious: there are many processes of thinking that we are usually not aware of, but which influence our thoughts and actions. Comparison is one example. Once we become aware of this process operating in the background, we make the unconscious process conscious.

Shared human mind: just as our hearts function in similar ways, our minds do too. For example, all our emotions are the same, as are our processes of thinking. To consider an analogy, computers share the same operating system, but the user is not aware of this operating in the background. Our minds are similar. What is unique about us is the content of our memory. The shared human mind refers to the 'operating system' that is the same in all human beings, so we can explore it together.

The 'I', the 'self', the 'entity': these terms are used interchangeably to refer to the sense of 'me'. I suggest that this is a creation of our thinking process, but we are not aware of this. This is the entity that chooses one over another, that decides what to record or not, and feels emotionally hurt. This 'I' also notices what is happening in our thinking process and is able to verbalise and share it with others. The mind that is meditating or self-aware also includes an awareness of this entity, the 'I' recording and noticing everything.

Recording: I use this term to indicate that the mind is constantly recording what it receives from the senses and records our thoughts and feelings, but does this in a selective manner, based on the importance that has for us.

Wisdom: a person who lives with this inner intelligence is wise and responds appropriately to every situation, including life's challenges. He or she has a sense of goodness, and lives with compassion and a sense of peace.